The Art and
Technique of
Analytic
Group Therapy

Commentary

"There was a style of reporting of psychotherapy that characterized the analytic impact: it was personal about the patient and about the therapist, and it emphasized individual human beings. The more recent emphasis on statistics and techniques does not make use of the personal style of communication. For this reason, this book evokes nostalgia: the person of a therapist is in it. This book speaks to the person of the professional psychotherapist and can help its readers gain perspective on themselves. It will be cherished."

–Jay W. Fidler

"This book tells us as much about the author as his techniques. A therapist to therapists, to beautiful and famous people, he prescribes himself in a group with consummate skill. Against cults and gimmickry, he sees groups not only as therapeutic but as a way of life, a kind of *raison d'être* of unlimited potential. I liked his style, his candor and wit, but most of all the nuggets of wisdom he dispenses, which make uncommon good sense."

–John A. Harrington

"Although the very personal way in which Dr. Grotjahn illustrates the artistic aspects of his conduct of group psychotherapy is the guts of this book, the clear and consistent conceptualizations underlying his 'spontaneous, responsive interactions with patients' should not be overlooked.

"The greatest virtue of this book is its openness and honesty, while retaining a strong sense of responsibility, which I think is not only a tribute to Dr. Grotjahn's personal and professional qualities but perhaps even more is the result of his deep involvement in group psychotherapy. His own development, as revealed in this book, is even more than the valuable section on the profile of the group therapist, the best testimony to the growth value of group therapy for the therapist."

–Steven H. Lipsius

The Art and Technique of Analytic Group Therapy

MARTIN GROTJAHN, M.D.

JASON ARONSON INC.
Northvale, New Jersey
London

This book is set in 10 pt. Schneidler by Lind Graphics of Upper Saddle River, New Jersey, and printed and bound by Haddon Craftsmen of Scranton, Pennsylvania.

ISBN 0-87668-252-2 (hardcover)
ISBN 1-56821-026-4 (softcover)

Library of Congress Catalog Number 76-22916

Manufactured in the United States of America. Jason Aronson Inc. offers books and cassettes. For information and catalog write to Jason Aronson Inc., 230 Livingston Street, Northvale, New Jersey 07647.

Contents

PART II
THE ART AND TECHNIQUE OF
ANALYTIC GROUP THERAPY

PART III
PROFILE OF THE
GROUP THERAPIST

Introduction

The working title of this book was originally *Clinical Observations.*
This title changed during the years of work into what it is now – *The Art
and Technique of Analytic Group Therapy.* It remained, however, my
ambition to describe the way I conduct group therapy: my style, my
technique, and my experience.

I have taken a long road to group therapy. Starting out in 1929 as
a physician, I began to specialize immediately as a psychiatrist. Seven
years later I had finished my psychoanalytic training in Germany,
where my father, grandfather and great-grandfather had been physicians. During my service in the United States Army, my practice
changed from psychiatry and psychoanalysis as I had practiced it in my
office, to wartime psychiatry involving work with many large groups
of patients.

After the war I became interested in the family as the cradle of
growth and maturation, of health as well as sickness. Out of this
project developed almost unnoticed my work in analytic group therapy. During these years of slow transition, I devoted much time to
working as a training analyst and this work turned into a study of the
structure, process, and dynamics of professional groups.

I will try to describe here how I conduct analytic group therapy, how I have learned to proceed, and what it seems to mean to my patient and to me. What I understand as "analytic group therapy" is defined in Part I, "Basic Concepts." These concepts can be traced back to my training and my work in psychoanalysis, to which I have devoted the major part of my professional life.

I was greatly influenced by the work of Sigmund Freud and, later, by that of Theodor Reik. At the center of Theodor Reik's approach stands what he calls "listening with the third ear," which can be defined as the role of intuition in the process of psychological understanding. There is nothing mystical about intuition; it is the preconscious perception of someone else's unconscious communicated by subliminal clues. If the analyst uses his unconscious as a perceptive organ for the collection of such clues, he will have learned to use his "intuition" as an effective and quite reliable tool.

Understanding starts from hints, clues, and hunches. It leads to insight and the inner vision of the unconscious. There is no specific analytic technique, or royal road, leading to the unconscious; there are only sincerity, honesty, and responsiveness. "What is heard with the third ear must be heard again and examined in the control room of reason" (Reik 1948).

I am skeptical about the language of technique. Speaking the terminology fluently does not mean understanding the meaning of the unconscious. Only in the courage to communicate freely and respond honestly and spontaneously, must the therapist be superior.

I am by nature and by training a therapist, not a theoretician. Throughout this book, my clinical orientation will be predominant, even in Part I which deals necessarily with basic concepts and theories. I want my readers to get an impression of how I conduct analytic group therapy.

My transition from standard psychoanalysis to family treatment and finally to psychoanalytic group therapy was gradual and natural – a logical outcome of my therapeutic growth. I started with a group of young, analytically sophisticated psychiatrists which was quickly followed by a group of senior psychoanalysts. I was then called upon to conduct group therapy with the entire medical staff in a psychiatric hospital. This was followed by group work on a closed ward of acute psychotic patients. In the meantime, my private practice was changing more and more to analytic groups.

I learned by experience and supplemented my observations through a study of the literature and by presenting clinical material and checking it with the veterans in our field. I was influenced by S. H. Foulkes whom I knew for many years, until his death in July of 1976. He was the founder of *group analysis* and of that kind of analytic group therapy with which I identify. His ideas about transference and resistance, his technique of treating small, slow-open, analytic groups, have fundamentally influenced all group analytic work. His colleagues, James Anthony, and P. DeMaré belong also to the pioneers of group analysis. We originally worked together in London and are connected by our publications and correspondence, our meetings and work.

This book has been written slowly over many years. It has been written with a double hesitation of which I was always aware. As I wrote I revealed a great deal about myself, as I do occasionally in my group work as long as it is not a burden to the group. I have applied this frankness, which perhaps could be called my style, to the group of my imagined readers. This book has been written for my "families," my groups, my comrades and friends, and those of my readers who want to know how I conduct groups.

My second hesitation in writing this book is as personal as the first. I have had a terrible time revealing group interaction and the private life of the group and its members. It feels like being disloyal to one's own family. With the help of all my groups, I have finally found a way to express myself about individuals and groups which shows my style, our interaction, and its interpretation. But personal, intimate details are absent or disguised, and all facts which would allow recognition have been totally omitted. The text remains true, but any relation to any factual person or group has been carefully disguised or eliminated. Although some may still believe that they can recognize themselves, their group, an individual of another group, or a specific interaction, only I know the persons and events as they were in reality.

Psychotherapy is an attempt to liberate the person's – or the family's – creativity. I no longer think in terms of healing. Nobody leaves my office or the group "cured" from being human. I hope everybody leaves it with a little more courage to go on, to climb the mountain, to be more himself, and to understand and accept himself and his neighbors.

The person who finally has the intelligence, courage, and honesty to be what he has to be – himself – is the free person, the existential man. Nobody can call him sick anymore, even when he happens to be different from anyone else.

Let me repeat. This is not a textbook of analytic group therapy. Its purpose is to give an impression of how I conduct group therapy and what I have learned doing it. The emphasis is on the style and creative effort in therapy, its artistic side.

The aim of treatment is to learn how to trust, to disclose, to develop intimacy without fear and guilt, to express one's self courageously, and to respond honestly and freely to others. Together with the strength to accept one's feeling of intimacy goes the strength to express one's hostility or aggression and to master it.

The dynamic or motivational nature of the therapeutic process is different in groups from that in individual treatment. While the individual has to struggle mainly with integrating his unconscious into his conscious, the members of the group have to learn how to establish a network of communication. This is the principal difference between individual and group therapy.

The aim of treatment is to become the person one has to be and to get started living and learning again. How this can be achieved will be described in the following pages.

Much trouble can be avoided in a discussion of group therapy when it is clearly stated from the beginning what kind of groups are being discussed. Dynamics are quite different in larger groups than in smaller ones. They are different in closed, open, or slow-open groups, in analytic groups, and in supporting groups. They are different in short and marathon sessions. Unless it is specifically stated otherwise, the groups discussed here are analytic groups, small in size, meeting regularly at the therapist's office once a week for two hours, occasionally losing or gaining members.

I

Basic Concepts

Introduction

The application of basic, psychoanalytic concepts to analytic group therapy helps to clarify the dynamics of the therapeutic process. The similarities and the differences between psychoanalysis and group process can thus be described and understood. In theory and practice analytic concepts change in character when transposed from the psychoanalytic situation into that of the group. This is why M. Foulkes, for instance, prefers to talk about "group analytic" concepts.

Psychoanalysis has definite therapeutic limitations, but is unsurpassed as a tool of research and training. In this book I will use this tool to show the dynamics of the therapeutic process in groups.

Analytic group therapy is based on analytic principles – for example, transference, resistance, and interpretation – and aimed at mastery of outer and inner reality.

There are three different kinds of analytic group therapy. One concerns itself with the psychoanalysis *of* the individual *in* groups as represented by Alexander Wolf. The second variety of analytic group therapy is psychoanalysis *of* the entire group as a whole, as represented by the technique of Jacob Moreno. The third variation of analytic group therapy is analysis *by* the group as developed by Michael

Foulkes, De Maré, James Anthony and others. It is this type of analytic group therapy with which I identify.

One major difference between the transference neurosis in the dual relationship of psychoanalysis and the multiple transference relationships in groups is that three trends of transference must be differentiated in the latter. The transference relationship to the central figure of the therapist is similar to the transference neurosis of psychoanalysis. The second transference relationship is extended to the peers in the group and forms an important therapeutic agent. The third transference develops in later stages of an analytic group process; it is the transference to the group as an early, preoedipal mother.

Analysis of the transference neurosis has become the focus of standard analysis. It seems that the fully developed transference neurosis is inclined to "swallow the analyst" (M. Foulkes). Dissolution of such a regressive transference neurosis frequently becomes time consuming and is sometimes impossible to resolve. Furthermore, such transference neurosis, modeled after the early mother–infant symbiosis, has a magic power, almost like hypnosis. It is mostly responsible for the ever longer-lasting duration of the standard analysis.

Anna Freud, in a dialogue with Michael Foulkes, considered such development a mistake, probably due to an unconscious need in some analysts, who want to be mothers and invite their patients to develop such regressive dependency. According to Michael Foulkes' observations, such transference neurosis is often stronger than the original infantile neurosis and is not just a mistake but an inherent danger of standard analysis. This has been recognized by analysts like Lawrence Kubie, who after a long life in analytic work, suggests a routine second analysis with another analyst to provide a chance to analyze the original transference neurosis. Franz Alexander suggested a realistic contact with the patient in order to lift him out of the residual regressive transference. In my opinion, the analytic group experience is the best solution for leftover transference residuals, as it does not invite any regressive transference neuroses.

I prefer not to talk about the transference "neurosis" in group therapy, but about transference trends or transference situations.

This implies that the systematic analysis of the transference and the transference resistance is neither possible in groups nor necessary. There is a built-in correction of the transference phenomena through the peer relationship in groups. An analyst is trained to let the transference neurosis develop to full bloom. The members in a group are neither trained nor willing to accept such projections for long and will correct them. This is the basis for the corrective therapeutic family experience.

It has been claimed that the therapeutic task in psychoanalysis and in group therapy is the same. I doubt the correctness of such a statement. In psychoanalysis the analyst's foremost assignment is to interpret the resistance of the individual against insight into his unconscious. In group therapy the therapist's assignment is to remove roadblocks in communication. The "unconscious" of the group is represented by that which is not shared communication. Thus the unconscious of the individual is different from the unconscious of the group.

The analyst in psychoanalysis is more or less a screen for the transference neurosis. The group is more like a "theatre-in-the-round" for the projection of the entire mind, conscious and unconscious. The mind is not a thing, it is a collection of personal images, of father and mother, brother and sister, of friend and enemy. The group, therefore, gives a more complete opportunity for the past to be projected into the reality of today.

In psychoanalysis the analyst interprets resistance against the unconscious, or against free associations. In group psychotherapy the therapist interprets the resistance against free, spontaneous communication and responsive interaction.

There are some group-specific forms of interpretation. The best interpretation in groups is spontaneous, responsive interaction. One does not need, for example, to call somebody hostile. The group's responsive confrontation to the hostile person offers the best interpretation.

There is another form of group-specific interpretation and that is *triangular interpretation.* For instance, a patient comes and complains about something and somebody in the group responds to this complaint. Then understanding interpretation may be offered by a third person who watches this interaction between the two antagonists.

The third group-specific interpretation I call *comparative interpretation:* the therapist occasionally compares two or more individuals in the same group in their similarities and differences and their dynamics.

Resistance in psychoanalysis is resistance against insight into the unconscious while resistance in the group is directed against free communication. This becomes most obvious in dream analysis within the group. It seems to me after years of observation that everybody in a well conducted group understands the meaning of dreams—except the dreamer himself. Most group analysts would agree with the correctness of this observation, which could be of the greatest import for the group process.

A question arises whether there is a specific form of group resistance and this seems to be the case. For instance, most groups in beginning slowly show what could be a form of resistance. When six to eight people come together once or twice a week for a session, they have to reestablish communication with each other before they can interact freely. What happened automatically in analysis with the greeting of the analyst to his patient at the beginning of an analytic hour has to be actively established in an analytic group session.

Something similar can be observed after a necessary interruption of the group sessions through vacations.

There is one kind of resistance which I thought could be observed only in analysis and that is the mutual adjustment between analyst and patient, but I learned that this can happen in groups too. Any group which has worked together for a year or two may automatically make some allowances for the peculiarities of one or another person in the group, as if to say: Let us lose no time by reacting to it. Such situations call for alertness in the therapist, who must interpret them.

The roots of group resistance may lead to the resistance in the individual. For example, when a person has overcome his resistance and begins to speak in the group after having been silent, then the entire group may come to life.

Interaction is much more dependent upon the freedom and the spontaneity and responsiveness of the therapist than it is in psychoanalysis. The group therapist must be turned toward the group. If there is anything wrong or inhibited in his relationship to the group it will be reflected in the behavior and interaction of the group. If the therapist has a resistance, the group will identify with that. In such situations the therapist must actively turn to himself and must try to analyze his resistance. Without that, progress will stop. The therapist is not a patient in his group, but it is his privilege and his duty to explain himself at times when the progress of the group demands it. He is not allowed to become a therapeutic burden to the group.

There exists a peculiar hierarchy of regression. In psychoanalysis therapeutic regression is controlled and slow and should be reversible. This is also the situation in small groups, but in large groups of 25 or 250 people an almost automatic, deeply regressive process begins almost instantly. Any group situation is a challenge to ego autonomy, but in large groups this autonomy is relinquished.

It has often been said that the free association of psychoanalysis is replaced by the free dialogue or discussion in the group. This is not quite the way I see it. The analytic method of free association is replaced in the group by the free, spontaneous, responsive interaction. This interaction is frequently more focal than free associations are bound to be. It is often asked whether my groups are problem-solving or interactive groups. In my mind this is not an alternative. Any group session may, and usually will, start with attempts at problem solving, out of which interaction then grows.

The longer I work with groups, the more I conclude that group therapy is the basic form of treatment. I no longer ask myself, "Does this patient belong in individual or group therapy?" My first question is always, "What kind of group?" There are many contraindications to analytic group therapy; this should not exclude a patient from other forms of group therapy.

When I have decided in favor of analytic group therapy I still have to consider the composition of groups. The family model is a good guideline.

Whether there are people truly impossible for productive group work is for me an unsolved question. I certainly have met people whose behavior in my groups led to the conclusion that cooperation between them, myself, and the group cannot be achieved.

There is one objection against group therapy which sounds convincing. It could be claimed that individual psychotherapy is one of the last small islands of freedom and individuation left to us at a time of mechanization and alienation, and that therefore individual therapy should not be replaced by the group. This argument is misleading, however, since the ego needs "the other" in order to form and grow in such a relationship. The group, more than any other situation, gives an opportunity for individuation. In psychoanalysis the patient is, so to speak, an only child. In group psychotherapy he is a member of a family.

Franz Alexander once compared psychotherapy to a corrective emotional experience. In this sense, group psychotherapy could be called a corrective therapeutic family experience.

1

The Transference

Transference dynamics in groups are quite different from those in the one-to-one relationship of standard analysis. Recognizing the tripartite nature of transference in groups provides a good basis for understanding their dynamics:

1. Transference toward the central figure, patterned on the transference neurosis in analysis
2. Transference toward peers in the group, patterned on that of the family neurosis
3. Transference toward the group as a whole.

In this latter transference, the group symbolizes the preoedipal mother figure (basic trust). It includes all the relations of every member to every other member, transferential or real in nature. It forms the background of the communication network, or matrix, which is essential to the group process.

TRANSFERENCE TOWARD THE
CENTRAL FIGURE

Three young women, all in the same group, developed three different kinds of transference toward the therapist. One of them was the oldest of seven children. As a child, she had replaced the mother and taken care of her younger siblings. She had fully enjoyed her privileged position, especially in relation to her father. She knew that she was his favorite and had developed that peculiar glow of beauty which one occasionally finds in beloved firstborn daughters. She established a similar attitude toward the therapist and enjoyed it fully without guilt. She had a natural maternal affection for "brothers and sisters" in the group. She combined her genuine motherliness with warmth and a truly feminine understanding of her fellow members. I appreciated it and considered her a great help in the promotion of the group's cohesion. Trouble started when her attitude of duty and devotion was not recognized by her young and inattentive husband. Insight into her habit of transferring affection for her father into the present helped her to correct her situation.

Another woman in the same group developed a quieter but similar attitude toward me. She had always loved her father and some recollections of happy times with him were cherished as the best moments of her life. She dreamed about a similar happiness with her therapist and enjoyed her dreams quietly and silently, knowing their meaning without interpretative help. As time progressed she began to analyze her relationship to the therapist and revealed how, with the help of her mother, she had become aware of her love for her father—an awareness resulting in great guilt and misery. She had succeeded without much effort in seducing her two previous therapists and now felt keenly the frustration of her transference toward the group therapist.

The third woman in this group was the oldest of the three and pregnant for the first time, while the two younger women were mothers of several children. She had a much more complicated attitude toward her father—an attitude of having finally come to peaceful terms with her still-living father, who, she felt, had made her life miserable with his negative, critical attitude. She felt that she would never appear lovable to any man. After a long struggle with the therapist, she developed some trusting affection toward him, then toward the group, and finally toward herself and her husband.

As in analysis, all three women could experience, analyze, and finally integrate the insights gained from the transference of their neurosis from the father to the therapist.

TRANSFERENCE TOWARD PEERS

Theresa was a young woman who reacted with shocked surprise followed by rage and envy to the introduction of another, younger woman into "her" group. She expressed her annoyance and hostility with great difficulty. She was envious of the younger woman's attractive appearance and self-assured, well-mannered behavior. Theresa doubted that "the other woman" needed or belonged in "our" group. It was only a short step from there to associating her sister. Emotions previously not felt were now activated and open for understanding and integration. The younger sister was the one who was supposed to have been "the boy in the family" and had succeeded in an aggressive, apparently masculine career. Theresa's peer transference to the new "sister" in the group mobilized her old conflict with her sister and bared it for insight and working through. She had been in therapy with quite a number of therapists, and the relation to the younger sister had often been analyzed. But the experience of the arrival of a younger "sister" in the family of the group provided a badly needed emotional dimension to the analytic experience.

In another group, a young man began to hassle a new member of the group and the newcomer reacted in kind, until both realized that they were reenacting in the group the Cain and Abel story both had experienced in their relationships with their brothers.

The therapeutic process is, however, by no means exclusively based upon transference and its interpretation. This becomes especially clear in a situation providing special peer pressure. For instance, in my groups I have rarely seen compulsive gamblers or people with severe drinking problems. However, moderate gambling as well as moderate drinking are frequent. My experience and my knowledge of the literature lead me to believe that the therapeutic benefit of individual treatment is limited for such patients. However, I have frequently seen gambling and drinking diminish among members of well-conducted groups. I attribute this phenomenon to peer pressure, sometimes silent but often outspoken and persistent.

THE GROUP AS THE TRUSTED MOTHER SYMBOL

A young woman, married for a second time, was being invited into the group. Since she was quite depressed, I introduced her myself and mentioned that she had tried to commit suicide recently. She felt unable to live up to the demands of her new husband and was exhausted by the move to a new city with new schools for her children. It all seemed too much to handle.

One psychotherapist, a member of the group, was loudly skeptical about the wisdom of accepting such a depressed woman in the group and brusquely announced that she was "much too sick!" The patient was angry about this rejection and, in spite of her depression, had the energy and courage to say somewhat haughtily, after several people had taken up her defense, "You can be reassured that I will not commit suicide as long as I am a member of this group." She kept her word and it seemed to us that it was not even difficult for her. She found in the group a good and strong, if unindulgent, mother.

Depressive people take well to groups, because a group will love them in a way acceptable to them. A group is neither threatening, overwhelming with affection, rejecting, nor judgmental, but offers the kind of support and understanding a depressive person seems to need and find acceptable. In other words, the group can take on the function of a well-meaning mother.

THE HOSPITAL AS MOTHER SYMBOL

Anybody who has ever watched the behavior of patients at a large psychiatric facility will be impressed by their affection or hatred toward the hospital. It is a mother—good, bad, or ambivalent; loving and protecting or rejecting; threatening or destroying. I will discuss below the powerful transference trends of psychotic people for whom a personal transference is often too threatening to be tolerated and for whom the impersonal institution is a better screen for the transference psychosis.

TRANSFERENCE TO THE GROUP AS A FAMILY

For many years I have been indebted to Dr. Walter Schindler's contribution to the literature on groups. He was probably the first group therapist to think of group dynamics in terms of the family. This model cannot be applied in a static way since groups are in constant change. Everybody will be father or child, mother or aunt, brother or sister, teacher or student, therapist or patient. All roles can be reversed or changed according to the unconscious needs of any member. It is this network of transference relations which S. H. Foulkes calls "the matrix."

A great part of the therapeutic process repeats the primary family situation as a corrective emotional family experience within the group. As a rule the group family is tolerant but not indulgent. The family may be judgmental, but an appeal is always possible. The therapeutic group family aims at a free, direct, spontaneous, and honest communication. Six or eight members hardly ever act as tyrannical father or domineering mother; there is always somebody who will take the side of a member in revolt and try to understand him. The family is fiercely loyal and forms the foundation for group cohesion.

Like all families, the therapeutic "family group" has a natural tendency to growth, maturation and health. It exercises a less pathogenic impact than a sick family does as long as the therapist does not impose his pathology on the group. No other individual member can impose his pathology easily. Thus the basis for a corrective emotional, analytic-therapeutic family experience is provided.

AN "IMPOSSIBLE" GROUP FAMILY

A middle-aged woman of undistinguished appearance joined a group which had worked together for several years. After three meetings she was unhappy and dissatisfied; she felt unaccepted, wanted to leave the group, and complained bitterly: "This group is exactly like my family. Harry behaves like my indifferent and strict father. Louise is superficial and dumb like my mother. Everybody turns to Josephine as if she were my sister, prefers her and listens to her drivel and fusses over her. Boris is my silent brother and you, my therapist, are nobody. I can't stand it any longer. Nobody notices me. I may as well not be here and that is that. Who needs this?"

It could be shown to this woman that she had within three weeks established herself in the group just as she had in her present and childhood families. The group and the therapist had to work hard and fast to show her how she manipulated her environment to her needs. This had to be done to prevent her dropping out. The group did not welcome her enthusiastically, but as usual, waitingly. We had reached the point of therapeutic confrontation: neither in her family nor in the group did she reach out for anybody. She did not fight for her place on the merry-go-round. At home she sat in a corner with a bottle of liquor; here in the group she isolated herself, was depressed, bitter, and resentful, yet still hoped to be discovered and invited. It was shown to her that she tested the group with her provocative behavior, and wanted to be accepted in spite of it. Our interpretation was taken as the first invitation to join us and as a first sign of understanding, if not of acceptance. Unlikely as it may sound, this group experience became a turning point in this woman's life.

A HEALTHY FAMILY GROUP

A woman in another group hardly responded for a long time. Under pressure she would participate in a rather meaningless fashion. She continually complained about her family and home life. She accepted every interpretation and every advice gratefully but followed none. No matter how often an interpretation was repeated it was accepted gratefully like a pearl of wisdom and then dropped. Finally I asked her why she continued to come. I did not imply that she should stop. She had made the decision to start, and I left the decision to end to her. I knew from her history that she came from a deeply disturbed and unhappy family. The mother was psychotic and had left her four children to themselves. The boys had run wild and the girls became depressed and confused. The patient repeated an almost identical family situation in her present life: her husband was always working and never at home, her sons were running wild, and her daughter was hostile and well on her way to delinquency. When the family occasionally came together, it was a wild, undisciplined, and confused encounter. It became clear that our group offered the first halfway reasonable family relationship the patient had ever known. She quietly enjoyed it and the group became an important experience for her. She did not want to use the group to change her reality at all. She used it to make reality bearable.

THE TRANSFERENCE SITUATION IN GROUPS OF ADOLESCENTS

Groups of adolescents show slightly different patterns of transference than other groups. Present-day adolescents are often brutally honest and direct enough to say clearly and without much hesitation what they think about their therapist. Any therapist who stands up against the sharp eyes of a group of adolescents has passed the baptismal fire. Young people of today have the sharp and jaundiced eyes of analysts. The next best test for a therapist is to conduct a group of his younger colleagues. Older colleagues are mellowed by experience and self-knowledge. The peer relationship is most important to adolescents; one-to-one transference, least important. Adolescents are quite resistant to the authority of parents or their representative in the control figure. They do listen to each other and the group can exercise greater pressure than the "voice of the establishment." An adolescent is almost honor-bound to protest against the therapist. It is easy for him to abuse the analytic situation as an active or passive hostile rebellion against which the therapist finds himself almost helpless.

The central conflict of adolescence is between the need for infantile dependency and the urge to individuation and identity. This struggle, acted out in the home situation and repeated in school and college, leads to the behavior problems that seem so significant to young people. The third transference trend (the group as preoedipal mother) shows all the features of this struggle, but the symbol of the mother has now been created according to the need of the group, providing a favorable therapeutic basis.

A well-conducted group of adolescents is no hour of rest but of drama and participation for all, including the therapist. Any therapist who tries to remain outside the process loses influence; therefore it is advisable in such groups to divide the function of the therapist between two persons, preferably a man and a woman. This has two advantages: first, it simulates the structure of the family and invites family transference, and second, the divided responsibility has a beneficial influence on the therapists' countertransference. The group process depends on the active, honest, frank, and spontaneous responsiveness of the central figure. The cotherapeutic relationship offers the freedom and opportunity to one of the therapists to become at times "one of the group," in order to sharpen his empathy, to interact, and to be accepted. At such times, it is good for him to know that the other therapist remains an observer and not a participant. There is in all of us an adolescent left alive who is a rebel, who is longing for dependency and searching for identity, independence, and individuation. There is in all of us a tendency to be mother and infant at the same time. Occasionally, tentatively and sparingly, we have to allow ourselves a partial regression. It gives us strength, patience, faith, and therapeutic impulse. This strength is sorely needed by the therapist holding onto his position in a group of adolescents.

A therapist may achieve in these groups more than a "countertransference cure." In treating adolescents, a therapist occasionally feels more intensely and perhaps also more frequently than in treating of adults: "Here by the grace of God go I, and I have to cure me in this, my younger brother." Such a relationship should be of transitory nature, and the therapist should be aware of it.

According to all evidence, analytic group psychotherapy is the treatment of choice for adolescents. A time will come when all adolescents will go through a psychoanalytic group experience, whether they are considered to be patients or not. Psychoanalytic group therapy for adolescents will become an integral part of growth in the education of free people of the future.

OTHER VARIATIONS OF THE TRANSFERENCE SITUATION

A special situation develops in the transference of hospital groups, whether conducted on the ward, or in the outpatient clinic as a part of the hospital's service. The therapist must know that such groups frequently develop a transference to the hospital as such, as prisoners sometimes develop a transference to the stone mother of the prison. Especially in the treatment of psychotics and borderline cases, such nonpersonal transference is of the greatest practical importance. For the psychotic person the transference is a psychotic one, which is more safely enacted in relation to the hospital-mother than to any individual therapist.

THE GROUP AS A COLLECTIVE PERSON

S. H. Foulkes once said, somewhat aphoristically, that the human mind is a group. Equally allegorically, the group is a person. Somebody in the group may act as a superego. Another member may delegate superego functions to somebody else in order to enjoy a temporary, guilt-free period.

It is easily possible to delegate ego and reality functions to the group. Frequently a member may turn to the group almost as if it were a jury and repeat in detail the events of the home situation as he experienced them in order to appeal to the group for judgment. Who is right? Who is wrong? Who is at fault? Who should be punished? And who should change? It is always tempting to project ego functions onto the group: let them tell me what to do, how to react, and what to decide. The group cannot simply refuse this assignment, it has to deal with it. Giving advice is more or less ridiculous. People know what to do. They have to learn why they don't do it and why they are driven to take what they know is the wrong way out. The group's advice is disguised interpretation. But this can be offered only when the given considers it neither as order or answer. I never give advice; I do give my opinion, hoping that it will be taken seriously. The person should deal with my opinion, not necessarily follow it.

Another member of the group may take it upon himself to play the role of a "personified id" or of the collective unconscious. He may do so consistently or occasionally. Such people associate freely, repeatedly bring dreams, or have easy access to their unconscious and occasionally show the breakthrough of the primary process. Their behavior can be used to ease everybody's access to the unconscious or, at the least, to gain temporarily this free associative liberty.

"THE MATRIX" OR NETWORK OF
COMMUNICATION

I needed a long time until I understood the meaning and importance of the "matrix" as S. H. Foulkes and De Maré have used the term. DeMaré (1972) divides group psychotherapy into three essentially different forms: therapy *of* the group (for instance, Jacob Moreno 1954), therapy focusing on psychoanalysis *in* groups (for instance, Alexander Wolf), and finally therapy *by* the group, as represented by S. H. Foulkes and DeMaré.

The individuals of any group operate against the background of a field which is called "the matrix" or network of communication and transferences. The matrix is a specific group phenomenon, formed by all manifest and latent potential relationships from members to members, transferred or real. Together these are the group matrix against which the group process takes place. Matrix is similar to the analytic atmosphere or culture or to group cohesion. I also sometimes use the term "group character."

No attempt to describe a group phenomenon is as distinctive as Foulkes' concept of the matrix, or network of intergroup relations. Foulkes considers free floating discussion or free associative interaction and spontaneous responsiveness as functions of the matrix. Guidance from the central figure can be reduced to a minimum once the matrix has been formed. De Maré states:

> If Freud had started his investigations using the small group setting rather than the individual's free associations on the couch, he might very well have arrived at his meta-psychological conclusions earlier than he did, since themes from group associations are usually far less disguised, far more dramatically transferred than those derived from individual free associations. The problem in individual analysis is the communication with the unconscious; the problem of the group is the communication among the members of the group (1972).

It would be a technical and methodological mistake to treat the group as if it were a collective which somebody could analyze like an individual. Foulkes has shown that the group's matrix enables the group to analyze itself and develop the necessary degree of free and honest, responsive interaction. Intercommunication occurs between patient and patient: it is perceived and interpreted by all and starts a "chain reaction." What is conscious to one individual may not be so to all. What is repressed to one may be obvious to others. Such an observation may be repeated daily in group psychotherapy. Somebody tells a dream, the meaning of which is unknown to the dreamer only, while everybody else reads the dream like an undisguised text. It is precisely this transformation of individual communication into a trans-personal dialogue which constitutes the therapeutic process of group therapy.

A BREAKTHROUGH FROM THE BACKGROUND OF THE MATRIX

It is difficult and perhaps impossible to demonstrate the matrix with a clinical example. I will try to describe an interaction from which one can conclude the existence and function of the matrix.

Liza had been in the group for more than two years. She was sent by her analyst, who continued her treatment but thought that the group experience would help her out of her narcissistic isolation. Her loneliness had become intolerable since her children had grown, and she was left alone with a husband from whom she felt alienated. The world seemed to her new, frightening, and not at all inviting. She remained silent for many sessions but then slowly developed relation-ships to the group. Occasionally she even joined the group for a dinner after the session. For many months she limited herself to moderately funny wisecracks, never taking anybody seriously and never being taken seriously. For a while the group tried to accept her with a silent shrugging of the collective shoulder as if to say oh well, that's Liza.

At the beginning of the third year, the group had changed. Some members had left and new members had joined. The new members were not willing to show the kind of indulgent acceptance Liza expected. The veteran members finally also grew impatient, and the entire group felt her presence a hindrance to further progress. I said to her that her irrelevant remarks were interrupting and misleading. Vivian took up the battle cry and said quite sharply that these flippan-cies had to stop. She was welcome to say what she had to say, but we were not here to interrupt our work or to be entertained by such nonsense. Knowing Liza's long history of alienation, I intervened, defended her, and said that her wisecracks were her first attempts to come out of her isolation and join us. To this Liza answered with a short outburst of hostility: "Stop protecting me. This is not necessary. It bores me." In her provocative masochism, she tried once more another flippancy to which now Ed responded, "You kill everything." He said it quietly, almost offhandedly. I was not even sure whether Liza had heard it, and the group proceeded.

At the end of the session I turned to Liza, having forgotten my irritation over her remark about being bored, and asked her whether she had heard Ed's remark. To my surprise, she and everybody else had heard it. They all looked silently at Liza who reacted with deep feeling: "Yes, I kill everything and everybody. This is my great fear as it is a fact. When I was twelve, I killed the son of my mother, the violin playing, concert giving virtuoso, a child prodigy dressed in a velvet suit. I told Mother that she could not turn me into that fantasy. She was shocked and so was I. She never dared to mention that prodigy-bastard to me ever again. He was dead. I killed him. I let her down, and ever since I have suffered under my guilt and lived in silent atonement." Although these were not her exact words, it was what she meant. Everybody had the feeling that she had finally joined us.

This clinical illustration shows the working of the matrix as well as it shows the interpretation of interaction in groups. The patient had been "bored" by me, because by protecting her, I had interfered with a painful but necessary confrontation leading to insight. The group had become her family, with a mother who wanted to change her into a fantasy boy and a father who tried to help her but understood nothing. The rest of the group symbolized her extended family, who, like the Greek chorus, knew what she herself knew all along.

Interpretation was not given by the therapist, but by an almost anonymous member of the group, who did not know the patient and her fantasy but responded spontaneously to her behavior and its influence on the entire group.

INSIGHT SPRINGING FROM THE MATRIX

A girl of twenty-nine, who wanted to be called "Honey" by the group, had been in individual therapy for approximately two years. Her therapist sent her to the group hoping that such group experience would help her in her "only child" attitude. She looked like a teenager, dressed like one, and behaved accordingly. She actually had successfully finished her studies and was a professor. The group decided to address her with her academic title which annoyed her greatly.

She played, as we call it, "ping-pong" with us, answering any question with counterquestions and noncommittal replies, as if hitting a ping-pong ball back. She always sat in the chair next to the exit and at the end of the hour she ran to remove herself from the group. I had to warn her that this was a tough, impatient group which had worked together for some years and had accepted only a few new members and that nobody wanted to lose any time slowly indoctrinating a new member.

I knew from her therapist that she felt uncomfortable and that she had not the slightest inclination to be "one of this family." She had been the only daughter of an adoring but authoritarian father and a silently suffering mother. Her academic career was identical with that of her father; she did what she unconsciously perceived her father hoped a son would have done.

At the beginning of the hour, I had turned to her and said, "I notice that you run from the group when the session is over and that you obviously avoid all of us as if we were a leper colony. If that's the way you feel, then perhaps we could give you a little more time and you could start your summer vacation now instead of in two months. You could rejoin us later in the fall. I don't want you to feel expelled, but perhaps you should have a chance to work with your analyst and try to understand your reaction to your first exposure to a group."

In an indifferent yet hostile way, she declined the offer, hardly speaking to me. During the next half hour, somebody would occasionally pick on her slightly: How do you feel? What do you think? Where are you? Do you hear us? She responded to all these invitations like a schoolgirl, attentive and bright-eyed but having nothing to say. The group talked about husbands and fathers. When everybody related their feelings about their fathers, discussion grew loudly emotional and insightful.

The right moment seemed to have arrived and to everybody's surprise, including my own, the girl responded with an outburst of wild hostility toward me: she confessed that she had felt deeply with everybody who had spoken. Then she turned toward me with unprecedented fury, calling me a Prussian, and an authoritarian, male chauvinist – intolerant, indifferent, always critical and, worst of all, sarcastic. She began to cry and wanted to stop, but it was too late. Through her tears, she described her German father, who obviously would have preferred a son and who had trained his daughter to be an extension of himself and a replacement for his hoped-for son. She tried to live up to his expectations, and gave up all her own feminine wishes, desires, and fantasies. She became an excellent student. Then one morning, rushing down to her car in an underground garage, to be on time to her early morning lecture, she was threatened and sexually assaulted by a man with a knife. She fought him off and screamed loudly. The man ran away when somebody else came down into the garage.

She turned to her father who flew into a rage and accused her of having provoked the incident. For once this was more than she could take; she screamed back through her tears at him. For a few days they did not speak to each other; then the father died of a coronary occlusion.

The story itself had been told to her therapist but not with such powerful, explosive, spontaneous dramatization. She repeated and then worked through the rape scene, especially through the rage against her father and her mother who had not defended her. She tried to settle with us, her new family, what she could not settle with the old one. After that we never called her by her title any more but addressed her by her proper first name which we had not known before. Slowly the group let her feel that we did not want her to be a male impostor or a sexually undifferentiated youth. We wanted her to be what she was, a woman.

In the hour of the dramatic recapitulation of the rape scene, she had become a member of the group.

2

Resistance

THE PRINCIPAL DIFFERENCE BETWEEN
INDIVIDUAL AND GROUP RESISTANCE

The main task of a psychoanalyst working in individual therapy is the interpretation of the patient's resistance, which is blocking access to his unconscious. The main task of a therapist working with a group is to interpret the disturbances in the communication and interaction between the group members. The therapist has to work with an essentially different form of resistance – one which stands in the way of honesty, trust, and direct, free associative communication and response between the different members of the group.

For instance, an individual may defend himself against the interpretation or understanding of his dream, which is unintelligible only to the dreamer but easily readable by the entire group. Someone who cannot understand another's dream may be blocked because he has a similar conflict or fixation and therefore a similar individual resistance.

The group resistance is directed against free communication, and not against the individual unconscious. A collective resistance may be caused by external circumstances which may interfere with free communication. For instance, the group may be in a vacation mood, or disturbed by some overwhelming social catastrophe or threat like the illness of the therapist, or by events like an election or other political development. Such an "inroad of reality" into the group atmosphere may look like a "group resistance." It is actually only a different focus of the group attention: reality has taken the temporary center of everybody's preoccupation.

There are, of course, also internal reasons for a resistance in the group communication. A death or a severe illness of one member may stop the proceedings temporarily. The group joins in a resistance against analyzing death fear and the danger of dying. The individual taboo may become general and thus a resistance to group communication. The birth of a new baby, especially when the proud mother brings it along and displays it for general admiration, may seduce the entire group into stopping the therapeutic communication.

There may be hours of resistance when the entire group has developed a conspiracy of silence after either a specific topic has been discussed or a specific individual has spoken. There may be sad news about somebody, and the group may feel that a silence is the only decent way to show respect and response. There may be some behavior in one individual which is so serious that the responsibility to react to it is silently shifted to the therapist. On other occasions something may be known to everybody but the therapist and nobody, as in school, wants to tell on another.

The individual's resistance is directed against the unconscious, the group's resistance against free communication.

AN INDIVIDUAL'S RESISTANCE IN GROUPS

Many patients working in the group may show as much resistance against insight into their unconscious as they would working in a one-to-one relationship with an analyst. There are, however, slight differences; for instance a group member may feel endangered or invaded and threatened by well-meaning interpretations and defend himself. Such anxiety is rare in group, defending one's individuality is less necessary there than with a determined analyst. Paradoxically it is, in my experience, easier for a patient to become an individual in a group than in analytic isolation. Here is an example:

Carl went to a meeting of salesmen and had a wonderful time there. When he got home he got into a terrible fight with his wife. He started the session by reporting the situation. As was his habit, he called on the group to function as a kind of jury who would hear his story and then pronounce the judgment: with a woman like that you have the perfect right to go your own way. He had, however, mentioned only that he had been out of town, but not that he had been with a girl. Another member clarified the situation with a suspicious question: "Did you meet somebody at that convention?" It became obvious to everybody but Carl himself that he had felt guilty about his adventure and, coming home to his wife (who had been caring alone for the big family), had arranged the terrible fight "in order to be punished." He would then tell the group and get absolution. The whole situation was so obvious, so clear that every member in the group understood it. But Carl needed some time to see what he had been doing.

GROUP RESISTANCE: THE SLOW START OF THE FIRST HALF HOUR

Another form of resistance in groups is the slowness of the first half hour. People need time and effort to shift from defensive, noncommittal communication to the free, spontaneous, honest interchange of an analytic group. Each time the session begins, all the members come into the room alone as individuals and have to become part of the group again. A group has to constitute itself each time it meets. The matrix has to be established, lines of communication have to be set up, tested and finally used.

I facilitate this process by not letting the group slowly constitute itself in the waiting room. I open the doors ten minutes before we begin in order to watch the group getting together in the consultation room. In this way there is no interruption of the group formation. Initial resistance cannot be overcome by the therapist taking the initiative. Whenever I used to do that, I prolonged the period of slowness. Speaking makes one an individual, and only later interaction can reintegrate him into the group.

OTHER FORMS OF GROUP RESISTANCE

The entire group may come late at times or they may start to talk about such difficulties as traffic on the way or parking. They are testing whether the communications are still working before they proceed in earnest.

I have learned to recognize the limited value of anecdotes. As a rule, they leave the speaker out of the group process. The group's response to anecdotes is usually indifferent tolerance. Occasionally it is possible to treat an anecdote almost like a dream and an interpretation can stimulate the individual and then the group to proceed from the story to the analytic "working through" of the group.

There are special difficulties in communication after a missed hour, and I conduct group sessions under almost any circumstances, canceling a session only when absolutely unavoidable.

In rare cases everybody in the group may seem to act according to a secret and silent agreement: Let us be good brothers and good sisters so we can indulge in the "good mother" we have created. Usually somebody's cry for help shatters the comfort and work begins. Not much analytic work is done when the group meets socially after a session or during the therapist's vacation. In such a situation the good feeling replaces interaction and serious work has to be postponed.

All groups have to learn that social taboos or well-mannered behavior must not be allowed to stand in the way of free communication and responsive interaction. I always make a point of discussing people who for some reason could not be present. Whatever we say behind somebody's back will be repeated sooner or later in different words as interpretation or confrontation after the missing member has returned. Talking about him, the group begins to understand him, and sometimes this is a little easier when he is not there. Listening after his return, he gets the benefit of the group's insight.

INDIVIDUAL RESISTANCE SIMULATING GROUP RESISTANCE

Individuals may endanger the group process with resistance arising from their own defensive needs.

A woman in one of my groups used "common sense" as a

substitute for understanding. Each time the group or I had placed somebody in the focus of attention in preparation of a confrontation, she rushed in and defended the patient before we could deepen our understanding. She was afraid of her own unconscious and projected this fear on other people in the group. She tried to short-circuit interaction before it could become effective.

There seems to be somebody in every group who prefers to be argumentative than to search for meaningful understanding. This form of resistance is especially frequent with psychiatric residents. Inevitably somebody says: "We all talk like psychiatric residents." Although this remark may be true and appropriate such a warning must not be used to undermine all interpretation.

If the entire group is up in arms against the therapist, he may safely assume that he has made a mistake. He may not have seen it at the time it happened and may not start to search in himself for his motivation right then, but he must try to analyze himself after the session.

SOME UNCOMMON FORMS OF RESISTANCE IN GROUP WORK

Among the many differences between psychoanalysis and analytic group therapy is the fact that nobody lies down during group sessions. Once in a while somebody may slide to the floor or lean way back in his chair. Usually this is not a good sign. It is a sign that the patient has retreated from group interaction into himself. In this way the patient slides into passivity, waiting for good things to happen. He expects the group-mother to feed him. Mothers, however, have the tendency not to react well to expectations. The group will respond by trying to get the passive member to interact.

MUTUAL ADJUSTMENT AS RESISTANCE

A cynical therapist is supposed to have said: "A cure in psychoanalysis is pronounced when patient and analyst have established a mutual adjustment to each other." The patient, after years of therapy, has finally convinced his therapist that his way of life, as crazy as it may be, is still the best adjustment he can make, and so the analyst gives up his ambition to change anything and agrees with the patient, who then feels understood. I have seen many such examples of mutual adjustment.

There are people who remain outsiders in the group because that is where they feel safe. At times the group, which may be busy with the active participants, may leave the outsider where he wants to be, on the outside looking in. I may take the initiative and point out the neglect by the group. I may give a special invitation to the outsider to join. On other occasions a group may accept a member as "the problem child" of the group. The attitude of the members may be tolerant and, perhaps, even indulgent, and leaving the problem child unattended. The court jester, the wisecracker, the flippant youngster may find similar places in their groups. It is as if the group shrugs its shoulders collectively like a resigned parent saying, oh well, that's Johnnie.

Mutual adjustment or a conspiracy of analytic silence is difficult to avoid in an analysis which extends over several years. In analytic groups open to new members, this danger is small; newcomers will challenge where veterans of the group have resigned.

Peter, who had been a member of one of my groups several years earlier, joined another of my groups for some additional work because of a crisis in his life. During the first two meetings he watched with interest and introduced himself when asked why he had joined the group, but in the third meeting he began interacting.

Then Mae felt "touched" by his interpretation of her defensive confusion. She had been out with different men every night for ten nights. The group did not react to her story since it was a report Mae had given frequently before. Peter turned to her and said: "I don't like your hysterical confusion, your insincerity, your dishonesty. Why do you live that way, that is terrible!"

Mae was shocked and said: "This is the best way for me to avoid intimacy and keep on going."

Later Peter turned to Anne and said: "I don't like your inappropriate smile. You come in grinning and then tell your sad story." Toward her too, the group had silently developed the attitude: oh, that's the way Anne wants to live; let her live that way. Peter's remark shattered her defensive facade, and she broke into tears. Her defensive smile did not hide her sadness. Both women were once more challenged and invited to change.

In the second half of the hour Peter turned to Liza, toward whom the group was by no means indifferent. Instead they were loving, accepting and supporting of her in the difficult situation of a young mother with two young boys. We always wanted to show her how demanding, strenuous, and stressful her situation was and that she should not demand more from herself than she was already giving. In this session she seemed especially fragile as she courageously worked on mastering her reality. Peter turned to her and said: "I love you." Liza was startled, and a few minutes later, we noticed that she was quietly crying. That somebody could love her in her "inefficiency," as she, her father, and her husband called it, was a great and corrective emotional experience.

GROUP RESISTANCE AS RESPONSE TO THE THERAPIST

It is ridiculous to berate the group when something goes wrong and the group process slows down or halts.

When a group is not interacting I ask myself or the group: "What is wrong today? Why don't we get started?" Often the group is responding and the reason for the stoppage lies with me.

Groups are sensitive to the mood of the therapist, and the analytic process in a group seems to be more dependent on the therapist than is the case in individual treatment. There is nothing else to do but to apply the same honesty and frankness as we expect from our patients in looking at ourselves. Such self analysis may take place right there in the group. At least it should get started there, though it may have to be continued later when the analyst writes his report about the session at the end of the day.

Self-analysis is rarely misunderstood by the group, but the therapist must not abuse it. This subject will be discussed in more detail in chapter 12.

3

Interpretation

Interpretations are aimed primarily at the resistance and only secondarily at insight. The interpretation is less often directed at the individual's resistance than at roadblocks in the free communication between the group members.

The clinical illustrations given here may sound to the reader as if my groups are frequently problem-directed rather than interaction-directed. We can spend considerable time on events and relationships which lead away from the group to the home of the speaker, to his marriage, or his business. In all my work, I try to keep close to the interaction but will never avoid looking at problems and conflicts within the individual or between him and his environment.

INTERPRETATION OF INTERACTION IN TERMS OF TRANSFERENCE

Since the beginning of the week, I had been feeling miserable with a cold. I cancelled my individual appointments but continued to conduct my groups. I have found group sessions should not be cancelled if humanly possible. One should guard the continuity of the group process with the greatest care. Individual therapy hours are not so crucial as the one weekly group session.

Tom and Karla were five minutes late, an almost unheard of event since they were usually early, sometimes twenty minutes early. They had good and bad news. The good news was that a lawsuit against Tom which had bothered him for two and a half years was finally settled out of court with complete release from further demands. The bad news was that the couple had had a terrible week of constant fighting. That morning they had both been waiting in the parking lot but failed to see each other. Karla had been angry all morning, having been awakened by torturous nightmares.

I thought I knew what was happening and said so. A week ago when Karla complained about a wart on her finger, I remarked how gypsies in the old country cured these warts and that I too was able to cure hers by "buying" the wart which would then become mine. She would be free of it forever. After the session I performed this treatment with Karla. This constituted symbolically a seduction by the father, culminating in the ceremonial payment of a silver dollar as the price for the wart. The scene was a dramatization of her central conflict with her seductive father. When she had been a pretty teenager, her mother had pushed her toward her father and then viciously suspected her of wrongdoing. Karla was attracted and frightened by this situation and repeated it frequently with father substitutes.

I did not apologize for this symbolization of seduction but used it as an emotional experience, leading to interpretation, insight, integration, and perhaps resolution. Working through her central conflict was supposed to settle it. It was amazing to see the change in the two people and in their relationship to each other, to me, and to the group. Tom and the group were induced to play the role of Karla's mother, but Karla was understood and not suspected, judged or condemned. Karla's anxiety and anger were her reaction to the guilt stemming from the seductive scene.

Then Rose got into a fight with almost everybody, feeling at odds with the entire group. Nobody seemed to like her. Even the newest member of the group, who had participated only three times, had already turned against her. Christopher, a mild mannered gentleman, expressed loudly his irritation with her and almost every member followed suit giving the reasons for disliking her as loudness, superficiality, submitting people to a cross-examination instead of reacting to them, bad manners and selfishness.

Rose then reported a "terrible dream" of the previous night: on her way out of a slum area she pleaded to be allowed to see the doctor but the nurse told her that she would have to throw a bloody dead rat at her before she could be admitted into the presence of the doctor.

Rose's situation and her relation to the group made it easy to show her how her provocative masochistic behavior and her almost ridiculous pleading "to be loved anyhow," made it difficult to accept her at all.

Rose was the second of two girls and she was supposed to be the boy of the family. She suffered all her life terribly under her fear of not being acceptable as a girl. She married a man whom she could offer to her father as his son. When she delivered her own son, she finally felt that she had given the father what he wanted and now she demanded his love and acceptance. To speak more specifically in the language of her dream symbols, she throws a bloody mess at the feet of her mother and says: "I did this for you. I give you now the son you never had. Now can I have the love of my father?"

The interaction was continued when Julie told her dream: a tidal wave was flooding her house. She could escape and was happy to see her children safe on dry land, but her husband had been drowned. She awoke with terror.

The interpretation according to our knowledge of her history and situation was again easily given by everybody: the tidal wave of sexual excitement threatened her existence as Antigone, the faithful daughter of Oedipus. She had been deeply attached to her father, left college to be with him when he died, married an invalid with whom she continued where she had left off with her father. Now, under the influence of the group, she began to get insight into her life as Antigone and wanted badly to live a different life which was forbidden to her by her loyalty, devotion, and the firm belief that she was bound to this man and the children "forever." Julie lived a truly tragic life. The dream showed the unresolved conflict between the wish to see her father-husband eliminated and to be swept away by the tidal wave of excitement activated by one man in the group. She became the most sensuous woman in the group, and the most virtuous one.

Later on the same day with the same severe and almost incapacitating cold, I saw a second group.

The session started with Magdalena telling that she was pregnant. It was clear to her that her conception was arranged by her as an angry protest against my leaving her and going on a vacation. This, the therapist's child, would be aborted, and she hoped to feel more kindly towards me afterwards. The group accepted her interpretation and not much could be added. I felt it was not the right time to go into detail about her intensive ambivalence toward me.

Then John wanted to hear from Otto and Martha, because they had talked so little recently. Martha obliged and told how she had worked her way out of the depression she always suffered when her parents were visiting. Not even the absence of her husband, who was traveling abroad, depressed her this time. She was happy to be enjoying a vacation with her children, who always made her feel good.

This was my clue to give an interpretation of her story: Martha's mother always abused her daughter and made her feel guilty for the mother's depression because she had not fulfilled the great ambitions the mother had had for her only child. Martha was supposed to live as if she was her own mother incarnate. Her husband's depressions repeated the situation and were taken by Martha as accusations by her mother. Her children showed her that she, Martha, could make people happy and could be loved.

Otto was angry about my interpretation, which he called "advice giving": "What kind of prescription is that?" Such "prescription" had endangered his life so that he did not know how to continue to live in or out of his marriage. He wanted to know two things but forgot to mention them while getting lost in a detailed account of his situation. Otto talked about his son who was visiting him and about whom he felt guilty. The only pleasant event in his present life was the sudden blooming of a deepening friendship between himself and John, a member of this group. It had begun by Otto introducing John to some of his business acquaintances in order to get him started in his career. The men compared their previous lives, unreliable fathers and sick mothers. Both men had had to take care of their mothers for years, especially during their early adolescence.

I concentrated on Otto's identification with the younger man, John, who represented what his son could not do for him and what Martha could not do for her mother – be a younger and better edition of himself. Otto saw in John the son he needed and John saw in Otto the father he never had. The group and I did not see any reason to interfere with this friendship which slowly died down after it had fulfilled its function.

Here Gertrude complained that she had had a horrible dream from which she had awakened with terror: she dreamed she saw a great group of people going into a cave, directed by somebody. She too went into the cave but turned back in time. It was clear that all these people died in the cave while she alone walked away. One man especially looked at her with indescribable sadness.

Everybody in the group understood the dream immediately with the exception of the dreamer herself and Martha. Only a week ago Gertrude had told us in a controlled but still tearful way of her escape as a child from Germany, while her parents went to their death at Auschwitz. Martha could not understand the dream because she too was an immigrant and had to deal with similar survivor guilt. Martha's parents were still alive.

At this point Alex got a severe anxiety attack. He felt he would die. He had responded to Gertrude's dream and to her story with his own death fear. Then he had realized that what he felt anxious about was his father who was dying in the hospital. Alex was deeply torn by visiting him daily.

A report like this does not bring out the full impact of such an anxiety attack taking place in the group, witnessed by everybody. When Alex suffered through his anxiety about his dying father, everybody participated with his own anxiety and his own feeling about parents and death.

A GROUP IN DESPAIR

A selected group of professionals had lost several members in the last month and no replacements had arrived. I had remarked that if we could not find replacements, we would not linger much longer but would terminate the group. I felt skeptical about the future, since two more members seemed ready to leave after several years of participation.

When the group began, Dick went into a long, pessimistic, and cynical report on the theme: everything is bullshit, absolutely bullshit: my life, my work, my research, my colleagues, everything!

The topic was taken up by Mike who joined Dick's devastative criticism. Mark continued with gruesome details about his second divorce, the trouble with his children, and the legal settlement, ending in general disgust.

I was tempted to say: "What are you talking about? For me not even bullshit is bullshit." However, I did not say anything because I had asked myself, "What are they talking about?" and had arrived at the answer. I said instead, "What we are doing here is bullshit. None of us wants to see that this group is now overaged, has outlived its rightful existence, and that we don't have the courage to act accordingly." I was not berating the group. It was simply a statement of my impression and response to their feeling.

The interpretation cleared up the situation, and after a short discussion, someone in the group asked to loosen the requirement for admission to the group. Then the general feeling became more hopeful and work was resumed.

Mike had been previously in analysis, but nobody could analyze his need to have a wife and a mistress simultaneously. His wife was the mother of his children; he respected her highly, while his mistress "turned him on."

He discussed the merits and disadvantages of several women with whom he had had pleasant relationships recently. The group was only mildly interested and soon grew restless and inattentive until I interrupted and said: "The details of these affairs do not help us to understand you. We are wasting our time." The remark stopped the group process, and after a short silence, Mike described briefly his almost fatal sickness as a boy of ten. Shortly thereafter his mother developed a personality change leading to a loud schizophrenic explosion followed by years of hospitalization.

Mike described the mother before and after his sickness and before and after her psychosis; suddenly it became clear that his need to have two women in his life had developed out of his relationship with his mother, before the break and afterwards. It was as if all through his life, he had tried to bring these two different images into one focus. The father had withdrawn from the scene into alcoholism, and the relationship with him was repeated in his relationship to me, the therapist: he treated me over years with studied neglect and indifference as if I did not count and as if I were not really present. Occasionally when I had tried to confront him and show him his behavior, he had avoided me but then called me later in the day and apologized for his behavior; he did not, however, change it.

This insight into Mike's love for two mothers was a turning point in his further development. He gave up trying to love one woman or two and turned to many simultaneously. He enjoyed his life without guilt or embarrassment to himself or others. He had taken good care of the mother of his children who were now all grown. He considered himself a man fifty years ahead of his time. Only in later years did he settle down in a new marriage.

It could be claimed that this clinical example illustrates the rather typical situation of analyzing one individual patient in the group. This is only partially true; the starting point of the interpretation was the restless boredom of the group with a member who was losing contact with us. The therapist, as the spokesman for the group, told Mike: "You bore us, you are not with us, you are outside the group." The result of my intervention was that he explained more of himself than he thought he knew.

THE TRIANGULAR ANALYTIC SITUATION

Joe was an angry young man; he participated as a member in a group of psychiatrists. He was caught in a hostile and always critical interaction with me, accusing me of being too charming, too diplomatic, and not directly penetrating and aggressive and, therefore, not really helpful. He bitterly complained that my attitude made any relationship difficult for him, as it discouraged the entire group from expressing hostility toward me and toward each other. I was in his eyes, a brilliant, narcissistic, seductive therapist.

I responded to the criticism without hostility, but explained my attitude as inviting and challenging, never seductive or teasing. My approach usually led me to the desired trouble area. I quoted Freud as having said once in a letter to Edoardo Weiss that some patients need a therapist "who fights for them."

That I explained myself at all, could be called "defensive," but all the members of this group were professionals who wanted to conduct groups on their own soon. I tried to show him how my approach worked, clearly admitting that it was based in my personality. At the same time I showed Joe, since it was the last group meeting before a three month vacation, a little of the benefit I had gained myself by participation in this group. I had learned to be more direct and confronting and less retreating from an eventual clash with a group of colleagues.

Charles, an experienced psychiatrist in the group, watched the two of us in action and then interpreted Joe's need to attack me as a way of avoiding intimacy and saying, "I cannot trust you; you are not perfect."

It was a good illustration of analytic assistance by a member of the group who became a cotherapist while I responded to an attack more as a person than as a therapist.

Such behavior on my part happens rarely and is almost always reserved for a group of "my brothers" or other therapists. I always feel tempted to make exceptions toward members of the fraternity.

The therapist who deals much with colleagues has to learn to resist the temptation to be right at all times and to be beyond critique. I found it difficult to eliminate the differences in countertransference reactions toward colleagues and toward other patients. I have learned my lesson many times and must continue to do so, since I too often forget we are all a little more sensitive to critique by colleagues—who know how to hit most vulnerable spots. A nonprofessional can never hurt as much as an unexpected attack by a colleague.

Ann was a tall, attractive, and intelligent girl: she was dissatisfied with the group and finding the procedure too time consuming said: "Shall I wait forever? When do we start? I am considering quitting."

I rushed to the defense of "my" group. I mentioned that we had lost several members recently and had to add new ones; that we were going through a time of preparation, which is not a time of loss. I continued with a few more explanations, until I became aware of my defensiveness and stopped abruptly.

A member of the group, who happened to be a psychiatrist, watched Ann's and my interaction and then said pointedly to her: "You just murdered two mental giants." He meant that Ann had calmly killed himself and me by threatening us with leaving.

Ann became thoughtful and responded with a recollection of an event which had happened shortly before she came to the group. She had "castrated a boy" who turned out to be a war veteran, and her senior in years. Her passion to destroy men was then revealed and demonstrated to her in relationship to the members of the group, especially to the therapist.

Her entire style of living was patterned according to the resentment she felt about being so tall. "I am not really a girl; I have the mind and the size of a man, his intelligence and his superiority. I shall show them what it means to be a man. I shall recognize only men who are so strong that they can survive my attack. I will not feel guilty, and then perhaps I can become a woman."

When I felt attacked and became defensive, another member of the group, less defensive, could calmly study our interaction, interpret it, and so open up the road to the material behind the resistance. This function of the third member in the triangular interaction is not limited to a professional member, as the following clinical observation illustrates.

A young, attractive girl told the story of her intimate relations with her previous therapist. There were all kinds of responses by the group, and I said, offhandedly, that according to my observation, any patient who seduces one therapist will try hard and frequently succeed with the next.

A young man took my remark up immediately with a sharpness significant for him. He showed that my remark could be "easily misunderstood" as a flirtatious and promising response to the girl's seductiveness. I had been totally unaware of this but reluctantly considered his interpretation as valid.

COMPARATIVE GROUP INTERPRETATION

The analysis of one person in the group can be of value for another and often for everybody. Equally effective is a comparative interpretation, which is a kind of exercise in "psychodynamic reasoning," as Franz Alexander called it. The value of such interpretation is twofold: in the first place it gives insight, and in the second place it is a training of the entire group in this kind of approach to mutual and self-understanding.

A well-working group got together one day with two women missing due to the flu epidemic. One woman was left facing a group of five men. Nearly at the end of the session I gave the following "comparative interpretation." It must be kept in mind that, as always, I do not take this report from a tape but from my recollection and from notes made about every group session at the end of the day. This is approximately what I said:

Big Bill has terrible anxiety about his inner emptiness. He fears he might have nothing to say or nothing to give, and so he avoids intimate contact, love, and friendship here and at home. He just wants to charm, since this is a good way to keep everybody at a safe distance. If a man lives long enough with Big Bill's attitude, he finally realizes his worst fear has come true and he feels empty of true feeling. For instance, Bill had defended himself successfully against Myron, with whom he had started a shy companionship which he then quickly dropped.

Carl is different. He does not feel empty but full–full of shit, that is. He displays his badness loudly and exhibitionistically so that nobody can overlook it. He wants to be accepted despite of his fear of being all bad. He is a "shit baby"; whoever touches him will become dirty–so he fears. He told us that in his childhood he liked to go into the park across the street. When he came back all dirty, and messed up, his mother was infuriated and punished him severely. There was no father to protect him. He comes to the group as to his mother from the park, shows us his dirtiness to test our love for him. He is an anal narcissist who reflects lovingly, not his face in the lily pond, but his anus.

Benvenuto stands in the middle between being full and empty. He feels half empty and is terribly afraid of continuing into the last third of his life without getting full. He tried to occupy the chair of the board of directors at five banks and has moved like a Roman emperor to conquer the whole world. He lives in New York, California, and Miami and nothing will fulfill him but the love of a woman. He still feels hungry for the woman with whom he can learn how to love. He is halfway there, having learned from bad experience.

Myron, whose last name is that of a little bird, lives like a European sparrow, sitting on the street under the horses waiting hungrily for droppings, which are his favorite food. He is a kind of anal Croesus–whatever he touches turns not to gold but into feces. His situation is hopeless but not serious.

There was not much time to respond to this unusually long speech. The few minutes left were spent more or less in contemplative silence.

Here is another example of comparative group interpretation. For reasons I do not remember, I put it in the form of my good wishes for everybody. I said:

If I could, I would protect Dora against herself. She has suffered enough from self-inflicted wounds.

I would like to be more affectionate and friendly toward Liza but she makes me feel like Prince Charming trying to eat his way through thorns.

Marlene has to be beaten out of her fake existence. I am doing better with her here in the group than I was with her alone in individual sessions where we talked about nothing. She is a fake from her hair down to her feet; even her speech is affected. She looks for clues to hit us with false or misleading interpretations. We all run from her and we may never see the true Marlene, if there is one.

I feel better about Henry since his wife is with him. We may get him to stop living in the shadow of his prominent father and start living his own life.

For Andrew, I would like to tailor a tight-fitting uniform, not necessarily a straight jacket but something which confines him to himself. If somebody has not enough inner strength to hold himself together then I like to try to give him form and restraint from the outside, to show him not to fly off the handle into histrionic behavior, but to turn to introspection, understanding, insight, and change. I like to help him develop that inner restraint we need to live with others.

Mike, Mark, and Dick arrived simultaneously, sat down, looked around, and thought, "Where are the girls?" While waiting for them I raised the question: "Is the group deteriorating?" Both girls, Eve and June, appeared fifteen minutes late. Eve was, as always, out of breath, claiming that she just could not make it earlier. June told us triumphantly and defiantly that she had come from an important engagement and implied that we should be glad she was here at all. My question remained hanging in the air waiting to be answered.

Mark summarized his experience of the past two weeks and then turned quite angrily on Dick: "I was on the verge of suicide. I was depressed as never before in my life, but nobody except Martin [the therapist] cared for me; nobody called. I could have perished and nobody would have known. You are all selfish, egoistic, cold, unfeeling bastards."

The group reacted nonchalantly to the outburst. Dick asked simply: "What happened?" Mark described the vicissitudes of his divorce which ended in financial disaster and the loss of both children.

I responded by saying something like: "Since I have known you, you have made nothing but mistakes. I am sorry to say that when you are down, but it has to be said. The first marriage busted, and so did the second. We all warned you but you didn't listen. When you neglected your two children, we warned you again; now they have turned against you and everything is in a mess. Every time you mention something from your life, it is 'magnificent,' but the end result is always disaster. You externalize your depression; you louse up other people's lives in order to find an external excuse for depression. This has to stop. Somebody said here once that we should not bother with trying to clear up the mess you live in. I agree with that. Let's start by cleaning up your inner mess."

Dick emphasized imploringly: "Listen to Martin!" Mike pressed the same point. Mark responded: "I have been depressed all my life. I have been happy and at peace with myself only once and only for five days in all my life. This was when I came out of the hospital after an operation and some nurse took care of me."

The group turned away from him. This may sound cruel, but it was the only thing the group could do. It turned Mark toward his inner reality and confronted him with his depression. The council of the brothers told him that it is better to suffer than to accuse.

After a few words by Dick and Mark, who both gave a kind of follow-up report from previous debates in the group, Eve began to complain about the man she was going to marry in four weeks. He had developed a retrograde jealousy. Otherwise there was great happiness and she had never felt so strong, mature, and happy as now.

My response: "I saw you when you were forced into independence after the death of your first husband. You developed a proud and fierce independence. You have lived as a free woman and enjoyed it. I would have liked you to enjoy that freedom a few more years before getting bound in marriage again – promising and happy as it may look."

For the first time June talked about her marriage, saying sadly: "My man saved my life but now he is destroying it. He liberated me from my prison and put me into his."

This description of the session gives the misleading impression that there was little interaction, that everybody stepped forward, made his speech, and sat down with my interpretation. However, everything said in this session grew out of group interaction stretching over many months and numerous sessions.

Karla had complained loudly of her senseless irritation with her husband, Tom, but now said she felt differently. She was also no longer troubled by her feelings for me, her therapist.

She told us one dream: at first she was angry at her parents, fighting and shouting at them. Then she went through the house checking the doors to make sure they were all locked. Her parents had never locked their doors.

Everybody in the group understood the dream. I summarized Karla's associations, the response of the group, my knowledge of her and her position in the group, especially in relationship to me: "You had a father you almost seduced and who played with you until your mother brutally stopped you with obscene innuendos. You now have a strong reaction to me, specially since we had some professional contact outside of the group. Now you seem to realize what has happened between you and all the fathers in your life, and you seem to be finding the way from your incestuous desires to the sexuality offered in your marriage. You are locking the door against temptations."

Tom, Karla's husband, reacted to her by talking about his sadness that during the Christmas holidays he was no longer able to go to church. "We both lost our fathers, here and in Heaven!"

From there the discussion turned to us, here and now, at the holidays, without religion, facing death and the hereafter all alone without faith or fathers.

I compared Tom's religiosity with my own development: we both had turned from neglecting mothers to our fathers. When Tom finally met his father on equal terms, he was deeply disappointed and turned to God for the answers. When I turned to my father, he made me feel accepted, and during the last years of his life, we developed a happy union to the detriment of my mother, who retreated.

Martin's reaction, I pointed out, was very different. He too had turned from the mother to the father. His disappointment was due to the undisguised hostility of his father and became a deeply felt hostility of his own and wish to murder him. It was this hostility which caused his fear of himself and of his unconscious. He defended himself against these dark threats with his attacks of phobic anxiety. They kept him out of situations which would activate his hostility.

Christopher could not turn to his father because he had none. He had to deal with his mother without the help of a father. He had developed a deep and fearful respect for the powerful and superior mother. He finally tried to settle his conflict with his mother by marrying women just like her in the hope of learning in his marriage how to master domineering women. The results were disastrous.

At this point in the discussion I felt that Gustave was trying to turn to me to say, "And where do I come in?" In this collective, comparative interpretation, I was not ready to include him, so I said: "I would feel completely at ease writing a book with Christopher, going hunting with Martin, or becoming a cotherapist with Tom and Karla, but I would feel uneasy going into business with you because I consider you 'a holy fool' like the uncle from Mars in the television show. You are so fragile, in my opinion, that I would not have the courage to say no to any of your projects. You are so sensitive, and you try so hard to be kind and generous that I would not know how to deal with you in the world of reality."

While Gustave withdrew with his gift of an interpretation, Rose reported a dream in which she feared losing her husband to another woman. She may have been more concerned with her newborn baby than with her husband. She was surprised at the great and almost ridiculous affection of her father for his firstborn grandson. It became clear to the whole group that her fear of losing her husband was a residue of the greatest fear of her life: losing her father's affection because she was "only a girl."

The group could show her how much she had changed since the birth of the baby and how much she enjoyed being a mother. She was no longer pretending to be what she was not, and was quite happy with what she was.

Neither the group nor I wanted credit for this change. The main event in her life had been the delivery of a healthy and happy baby boy. He has shown his mother that to be a woman has its rewards, and the affection of her father and of the group has shown her that we are willing to accept her as a woman. Her depression was a reaction to the loss of the boy in her. Now that she had given life to him again through her son and had largely delegated her masculine traits to her husband, she had become a woman. Nevertheless, she still had some doubts whether she deserved to be loved as a "woman only," as the dream symbolized.

4

A Remark on Regression

The nature of every group, as well as the nature of the psycho-analytic situation, implies an invitation to regression. As in sleep or the first step of a creative effort, regression may take place, as Kris once said, "in the interest of the ego." Regression in groups is of a special nature, as was pointed out by Sigmund Freud in *Mass Psychology and the Psychology of the Ego.*

Membership in a small group is a symbolic invitation to assume the place of one of the children in a family. Superego and, at times, ego functions are projected safely onto the therapist or outside the group. This allows unparalleled freedom of expression. The method of free association in psychoanalysis is partly replaced by free interaction among all the group members and partly by free and spontaneous responsiveness.

There is a kind of benign, competitive, and reversible regression in a group. The primary process becomes visible and understandable yet does not threaten. This benign therapeutic regression is perhaps the reason why groups need not convene daily, as in individual analysis.

"Competitive regression" – a fortunate term coined by Semrad – is the reason why people in groups are in contact with each other's unconscious. The individual patient has to reestablish this therapeutic regression each time he lies down on the couch, while competitive regression takes place almost automatically once the group forms at a meeting (Scheidlinger 1968).

II

The Art and Technique of Analytic Group Therapy

Introduction

I have not attempted a comprehensive coverage of analytic group therapy here, but instead have selected only significant specimen situations to give an impression of the way these groups operate. The personal nature of my observations will be emphasized at all times.

In chapter 5, the preparatory work will be described which takes place with individual patients before they are ready to join a group: diagnostic interview, individual therapy, establishment of the therapeutic alliance, laying the groundwork for group therapy, which is an unlimited, free and spontaneous communication between the patient and the other group members. The importance of selection, ground rules, and physical set up will then follow. Chapter 6 will deal with questions of starting the group proper.

In chapter 7, I will describe special situations that arise when the group is in progress such as the inroad of reality into the meeting, clinical illustrations of the group in process, the special situation of married couples, and the dynamics of acting out. Chapter 8 will be devoted to such problems of termination as assessing it as a sign of resistance, determining success or failure, and setting dates for graduation. Special attention is paid to the problem of dropout patients.

My groups consist of six to eight people meeting two hours, once a week; they are slow-open groups – groups meeting over long periods of time, aiming at free communication. As I try to describe the way I conduct analytic group therapy, the high degree of psychiatric sophistication of my groups must be remembered. Three-fourths of my patients in September 1972 had previously undergone psychoanalysis or intensive psychotherapy by analysts; only one-fourth had minimal or no psychotherapeutic experience.

5

Preparation for the Group

The preliminary individual interviews between patient and therapist before group therapy starts have several aims. The main point is to establish a working alliance between the two. During these interviews, the patient is given a model of interaction. The interviews are aimed at establishing trust and courage for confrontation and interaction. I consider this working alliance the starting point of group work. The relationship between the therapist and the patient will remain open to include the group later. Individual sessions prepare the patient for the repetition of the primary family situation in the group. A good working alliance with the therapist facilitates transition into this group situation.

The goal of therapy is to help the patient to love and work again. I should also include the ability to play as a necessary function for the healthy enjoyment and experience of being alive. To reach this goal, and understand himself and others, the patient must be brought in contact with his unconscious.

INDICATIONS

The basic part of all therapy should take place in groups. I believe group therapy is the basic model of treatment, the primary therapy, everything else being secondary.

There will always be a place for personal interviews. When the patient goes to a therapist he must be seen alone for the first interviews. The aim of these interviews is to clarify what Franz Alexander called a "dynamic reconstruction" as a basis of understanding and treatment. The better therapist remains open-minded to changes in the dynamics, adding details as the therapeutic relationship deepens. These first consultations are concurrently therapeutic sessions during which interaction and transference between patient and therapist begins. I no longer ask the question, "Group or no group?" I ask, "Which group? And when to start?" Indications and counterindications have become a question of the composition of groups.

THE COMPOSITION OF GROUPS

There is an enormous variety of groups. With every different group, a variation of technique develops according to the group's needs and the therapist's style.

Groups differ on the basis of size and frequency of sessions. There are differences according to meeting place; groups may meet in private offices, hospitals, out-patient clinics, churches, business offices, research or recreation facilities, basements, or on a Mediterranean cruise.

I even think that the old fashioned psychiatric hospital rounds should be replaced by daily group meetings of the entire ward including medical and nursing staff. Such groups would not satisfy the therapeutic needs of individual patients and should be supplemented by smaller groups.

There are other variations of groups: they can be classified according to the time spent in sessions: forty-five minutes or two hours. I prefer full-length sessions in which the two hour period can be extended to three or four hours.

Groups may be arranged according to age of the participants. There are groups for children, or adolescents, who do better when working together. Old people may have to meet in their own groups by necessity.

Other groups may be defined by the patients' presenting symptoms: alcoholics, homosexuals, criminals, schizophrenics, depressive suicidal patients. It is advisable to keep hypertensive or coronary patients together, as well as obese persons who do better in groups with each other. Obstetrics wards and postnatal care units could learn much from group techniques. After all, the first experience with group started on the wards of a tuberculosis sanitarium.

There are groups defined by marital status: singles, married or unmarried, couples, or families.

There are open and closed groups. I prefer slow-open groups from which people graduate and to which new members are added. This arrangement has the advantage that newcomers learn group communication without the kind of instruction necessary when everybody is new.

I can also recommend "holding groups." I have found that waiting lists are a cruel institution and should be discontinued. People should be taken into groups immediately. Patients can be studied in the holding group and then assigned to permanent groups as space becomes available. Holding groups have great predictive value.

It must be kept in mind that every difference in groups and every variation of technique is also expressed by a change in the transference.

Variety in the composition of groups is not exhausted by this list of possibilities. Not mentioned here are groups of patients and their families meeting during visiting hours in hospitals. Only with such groups can one really see schizophrenia as a sickness of the family. Groups of relatives may have great therapeutic impact.

The majority of psychotic patients do not belong in private therapy as conducted in private offices. The treatment of most psychotic or addicted patients should be centered in hospitals or outpatient clinics. Most psychotic patients belong in day centers, halfway houses, or outpatient clinics. This can be understood in terms of transference. A transference psychosis to institutions can be better utilized than one to an individual therapist.

There is one more group in the planning stage: it is a wishful fantasy I have not yet realized. I plan to set aside time during my working week for a "drop in" afternoon, where people could react spontaneously and freely, presenting their problems to strangers in order to benefit from their responses and interaction. Every member of all my groups would be invited to participate.

THE SMALL SLOW-OPEN ANALYTIC GROUP

Finding the right group is important, but it involves an enormous number of aspects. It is often good enough to find a group which fulfills some of the requirements. I do not hesitate to invite a patient to a group just because I need a man or a woman in that group to replace somebody who has left. Fulfilling such needs for the group gives the patient a good start.

Neither do I hesitate when a patient says he can come only on Tuesday evening. I will accept him into the Tuesday evening group. Such realistic arrangements work out well even in the irrational psychological atmosphere of later work. I have only rarely seen disadvantage for this method.

I do not go so far as some of my colleagues who claim that a newcomer is the problem of the group, not of the therapist or the individual patient. I take full responsibility for the placement of the patient. I take the realistic arrangements seriously, while considering the group and its needs. I put much energy into facilitating the integration of the newcomer into the group. At all times I am aware of my responsibility to make therapeutic work possible.

I know it sounds provocative, but it is nevertheless true that a pretty girl is welcomed by any group, while a domineering, controlling, and scheming person will find instant antagonism from everyone. It helps the therapist compose the group if he thinks in terms of creating a group family. A group of unrelated people will not work well or at least will need a very long time to get the group process started and show results.

The orchestration of the group is an art, like picking and arranging flowers or coordinating the composition of a harmonious orchestra which can work well as a team.

WHEN IS A PERSON READY FOR GROUP THERAPY?

When I started to work with groups, I invited a new patient to join only after I was well acquainted with him and thought I could reconstruct the dynamics of his development and of his neurosis. I also thought it would be better for him and the group if he would know me and my way of working and speaking.

During the years, I have changed my attitude and the time spent on individual work is getting consistently shorter. Some patients now come directly with the outspoken wish to join one of my groups and do not need much time for preparation.

I consider a patient ready for groups when he begins to express himself spontaneously and when I have reason to believe that he is willing to listen to the members of the group, knowing that their conflicts are his too. He should not consider the group's responsiveness as an attack which calls for defense even if the group should be aggressive or hostile. He should try to consider a confrontation as an opportunity for insight. Anybody consistently on the defense who does not give himself the chance to learn is not yet ready to join a group; if he tries anyway, he will soon experience confrontation. The patient must have learned to a modest degree how to proceed in the face of resistance.

In other words, a patient is ready for the group when a working alliance has been established between him and me and when he is willing to enlarge this alliance by including the group family.

THE QUESTION OF GENETIC MATERIAL

Even while the group focusses on the here-and-now, it still considers the past and future. In the preliminary individual interviews it is my goal to get an impression of the patient and to be more or less ready for a psychodynamic reconstruction. Perhaps as a result of years of psychoanalytic practice, I do not feel at ease with the patient if I do not have enough genetic material to offer at least myself a genetic reconstruction of his development. I have, however, learned to reconstruct this motivational history much more rapidly than I used to. It is possible I will be able in the future to do this while working with the patient in a group. It would be an advantage if the group could witness my getting acquainted with a patient at the time he joins the group. I have had some experience observing groups in which I did not know anybody, and I was astonished at how well I could recognize the central conflict of the different group members.

After a few preliminary individual interviews with a middle-aged, depressed and angry woman, I could easily reconstruct her dynamics: she had been a good baby, a good daughter, a good wife, and a good mother. She claimed to be tired of always being so good and then proceeded without delay to try to be a good patient until she realized that to be good was not enough. She had to learn to be less good to everybody and better to herself. Having been able to grasp the dynamics of this woman's depression in such general outlines, I felt that I understood her sufficiently to have her work in a group. I invited her to a group where she would find a "sister" of hers, who already had a head start in her rebellion. She also would find another woman who could serve for her as a model of a mature, free-living and creative person who was just finding out how to work on her marriage problem. One of the men, quite similar in character and profession to her husband, would enable her to learn some of the infighting she had so carefully avoided all through her life at home. There was also a man young enough for her to reenact many of the feelings she had toward her grownup son. The patient took to the group like a carp to water and her liberation influenced even the behavior of her husband, the Rock of Gibraltar.

INVITING THE PATIENT INTO A GROUP

Many therapists find it difficult to guide a patient from individual therapy into accepting the group. Like so many other problems I found that this is often a problem of countertransference. If a therapist is ready and thinks that this patient belongs in a group, he will find no difficulty convincing the patient without undue pressure. Occasionally I have to point out that I have no patients in individual therapy only, and that I always combine both forms of treatment with the goal of having the patient in groups only, without marginal interviews. At all times, however, I analyze the resistance to joining the group – in the patient and in me.

Every patient dreams about being his therapist's only child and hoping to have found the ideal parent who listens and loves. The therapist may be tempted to respond to this wish with the fantasy of being the good parent. This wish to be an only child has to be analyzed and many patients, especially in recent times, have replaced this fantasy with the unconscious wish to join the "ideal and perfect family" of the therapist as his favorite child.

6

The Starting Group

When I see patients in individual interviews, I always see them in my consultation room which is at all times set up for group sessions. I believe it is not right to have an analytic consultation room which has to be changed for group meetings by pulling out bridge chairs from a closet or from under the couch, as I have seen it being done.

When a patient visits me for the first consultation he sees the analytic couch with my chair behind it and the circle of seven comfortable chairs, each one provided with a little footstool. Patients realize the symbolic meaning of this arrangement. The empty chairs symbolize the silently waiting group.

Beside my chair stands a small table holding the clock, the calendar, my schedule book and some notepaper. Every person is fully visible. There is no division between "above the table" and "under the table."

I try to aim at a medium between comfort and asceticism. All the chairs are comfortable but not heavily stuffed, which is too soporific. Perhaps the footstools are a remnant of my European background. People are often startled by them and have suspected them to be mousetraps or microphones, but no one has ever refused to use them.

There is a slight hesitation at first, but after the first session, nobody sits down without fishing for one of them, even if he has to reach under somebody else's chair. All my chairs are on little rollers and allow people to move or turn in any direction.

The asceticism of my office is emphasized by the lack of art objects or pictures; nothing decorates the walls except my books which cover the wall behind me. If I were to rearrange my office, I would move the library into another room; I like my walls to be free of any distraction since I visualize what I hear on the walls as on a screen. I would remove any reading material from my waiting room to emphasize that the session begins there and that nothing should distract anybody from contemplative preparation.

I prefer not to distribute the group over the office but to keep them together – almost physically in touch with each other. I no longer hear with the sharpness of a young man, and in our profession, a hearing loss so slight it can hardly be detected by testing is a hindrance. Such a handicap can be overcome by the physical arrangements and by a hearing aid.

For reasons incomprehensible to me, adolescents prefer to sit on the floor. A friend of mine running a mental health center with ample space for many groups was worried about the expenses for furniture; he was enormously relieved when he noticed that he needed no furniture at all since all the students draped themselves picturesquely on the floor.

A MINIMUM OF GROUND RULES:
THE TIME ELEMENT IN THE GROUP SESSION

All my groups are scheduled for ninety minutes; however, I have the tendency to start early and to finish late so that an average session lasts two hours. I always open the doors to my office ten minutes before the appointed time in order to keep the group from forming in the waiting room. I want the group to form in front of my eyes since their distribution gives me clues about the relationship among the peers and about the transference. Their small talk as they get together also gives me various hints.

Groups proceed according to a peculiar timetable. It is rare that much interaction happens immediately or that an interpretation is needed during the first half-hour, although one is occasionally given. As a rule the next hour is better and more productive for the group process. I know therapists who therefore try to concentrate on the last half-hour and who feel tempted to and actually conduct a shortened group meeting of only forty-five minutes, hoping that it will represent the last forty-five minutes. In my opinion this is not possible. Like a meal, a group session should not be rushed nor should it start at the end. The group process should take its course slowly, spontaneously, freely, and without undue pressure. Even though I am always trying to shorten the time of initial resistance, I never try to hasten the course of a session. Actually the term *resistance* applied to the first half-hour of slow interaction is not correct. This is a time of preparation and of taking position in order to clear the field for response, interaction, and insight.

A FOOTNOTE ON SMOKING

A group therapist needs all his attention to watch the group and to respond to the interaction. I even consider smoking a distraction, so I always try to limit smoking in my groups. Pipes and cigars are simply not permitted, and cigarettes are so criticized that the majority of groups are kept free of all smoking. I discovered several times that some members were smoking only during the group session and not otherwise. I did not hide my annoyance but tried to analyze the defensive nature of such behavior. The group exists to feel and study inner tension, not to let it go up in smoke. Recently I have instituted a no-smoking rule in all my groups.

As a carryover from analytic practice, I do write it down whenever somebody reports a dream. However, even then I do not take detailed notes but only write down the name of the dreamer and a word or two about the dream, to help me later reconstruct it. In my experience, the dreams told to the group are more easily forgotten than any other part of the group process.

I consider it of the greatest importance to report briefly in writing about every group session. It is easier for me to write these reports half a day later than immediately after the session. I never have conducted a group or participated in other therapists' group work as a consultant without writing approximately a one-page report about it.

MONEY QUESTIONS

It may appear to the outside observer that group psychotherapy is an easy way to get rich. Six or eight patients can pay more than almost any patient is willing to pay individually. While this is factually true, it does not work out that way in practice. In the first place, it is doubtful whether anybody can or should carry more than two groups during one working day. I know of therapists who carry more, but I do not recommend it and I do not do it myself. I suggest on the contrary maintaining an easy and free schedule. For me it is necessary to have at least one half-hour of free time before I start a group. I cannot always arrange my schedule in this way, but I insist on it most of the time. I also avoid seeing an individual patient immediately after a group session. I prefer to take a walk, to do nothing, or to busy myself with anything but therapeutic work for an hour after each group session. Half of my groups are so scheduled that after the people leave my office, I too leave.

In my experience, the members of the group are more reluctant to pay than in individual therapy or in psychoanalysis. Group members pay more slowly, not as promptly at the beginning of the month. It is easy for an analyst to make it clear to the patient in analysis that he resists payment and that this has to be analyzed, since it would be the end of further treatment if an honest attempt were not made to pay bills promptly. No group therapist finds it easy to stand in front of the group and to discuss members of the group who have not paid. I have no special hesitation to do so, but I find it difficult to repeat my request.

The discussion of money should remain a group problem and not an individual one. I consider it a mistake to delegate the financial arrangements to an accountant or a secretary unrelated to the group process, especially today when money is such an important symbol. To leave it out of the group process would constitute a grave technical mistake.

The group family is inclined to assume that "Daddy has enough money," or "The others will pay." I also found that frequently patients who drop out of treatment do so after building up a handsome collection of unpaid bills.

THE HANDLING OF CONSULTATIONS

Even during my work as an analyst, I always was quite free in allowing patients to cancel without being charged. I know all about resistance and analyzing it, but I still do not feel quite right in charging analytic patients for service not rendered. Furthermore, since I believe in the maturing influence of travel, whenever a patient wants to go on a trip that doesn't coincide with my own vacation, I am in favor of it. The situation is different in the case of canceling from a group session and I do not allow it. I will bill every member of the group according to the number of sessions the group had during the month. I also expect members to let the group and me know when they cannot attend so that neither I nor the group worries unnecessarily.

There are times when it is doubtful that a group should meet or not, for instance between Christmas and New Year's or the evening before a holiday. Occasionally I offer to be present if at least three group members are willing to attend. I do not mind working occasionally with smaller groups. A good mother is always there for her children to come home to. This does not prevent me from taking three months for my annual vacation. I try to avoid all other cancellations on my part. I have found a group is more difficult to start after such interruption than an individual.

GROUP SPACE AND THE GROUP'S "BODY LANGUAGE"

I have always been aware how much a patient can express by the chair he chooses as his place within the group. There is a certain group space which speaks as loudly and clearly as the body language of an individual.

To my right usually sits either my right hand man, Daddy's little helper, or somebody who wants to sit under the protective wing of the mother-hen. The chair to my left is usually taken by somebody who considers herself my favorite. Unfailingly, the opposition sits straight across the room, facing me directly. In the far left-hand corner sits the person who has decided to watch from the sidelines and who waits for a special invitation to join. The newcomer prefers to sit close to the door in the far right-hand corner as if to show he has not yet entered and wishes to keep the road to retreat open.

The person who wants to watch before he is seen himself sits with his back to the window while somebody who wants to be seen in the right light may choose his seat facing the light of day.

If a patient suddenly changes place, it indicates a change in his transference relations.

SAFEGUARDING THE CONFIDENTIAL NATURE
OF THE GROUP PROCESS

Whenever I introduce a new member into the group I repeat the request to keep everything said in the group, every interaction, and all information about participants as strictly confidential. What happens in the group is nobody's business outside of the group. While ostensibly addressing the new member, I know that I am heard by everybody. In the years of work with many groups, I have hardly ever had reason to be disappointed in the ability of everybody to honor this obligation to confidentiality.

There were a few exceptions. Once a physician, who certainly should have known better, told another physician about members in one of my groups. He explained that at that moment he had considered himself as a physician talking with a colleague about an interesting professional situation and not as a patient. This explanation was accepted, but it did not free him from having betrayed confidence we had in him.

The request to keep group procedures strictly in confidence should be repeated when a member has announced his intention to leave the group. Then I repeat once more the request to honor privileged group communication. Leaving does not bestow the right to report anything.

I once had a man in a group known to everybody through his public role. He was naturally concerned that somebody would go home and say that they had met him in the group. A few weeks later this man was interviewed on one of the nationwide television talk shows. He came dangerously close to the borderline of indiscretion and almost betrayed the confidentiality he had demanded so loudly from others. He talked freely about his group experience and the therapist, how deeply impressed he was and how favorably it compared with his previous therapy. However, no personal details were revealed by him at any time and nobody felt betrayed.

It seems to me as if the confidentiality of the therapeutic process has become a fetish in analysis. People do not mind revealing their innermost secrets when they have made themselves familiar with the members of the group and begin to feel a part of this group. Sometimes this happens long before they really have established themselves in the group. Such early revelations are at times a plea by the individual for group acceptance. It is as if these people who so freely talk during their first confrontation with the group were sending out the message, "This is the person I am, please accept me as one of you." The request for confidentiality is related to the outside reality of the group, but there are no frontiers drawn between the different members of the group. Secrecy is not possible within the group, while it is necessary outside.

STARTING A NEW GROUP AND STARTING A NEW MEMBER IN A SLOW-OPEN GROUP

To start a new group with six or eight people is the most difficult assignment for the therapist. It is much more difficult than placing a new member into a slow-open group. Such a new member only needs a few introductory remarks and few words about ground rules; everything else he learns as he goes along. The best preparation for the group is by the group.

It is rare that a new group comes to a therapist already composed as a group. It happened once to me that six young psychiatrists in training declared their intention to work as a group with me. Another time a group of twelve people came to me, having lost their therapist through death. Whenever I took over such a ready-made group it turned out well.

There are occasions when a group therapist has to form a new group from the individual patients of his practice. The nucleus of such a group is each individual's working alliance with the therapist. When all my groups are filled and I have the need to start a new group, I begin with at least four members. I know that the additional two to four members will be found within a short time. I introduce each member individually, with a few words about the ground rules, mostly concerning confidentiality and punctuality.

In my practice it is rare that I find unanalyzable resistance against participating in group work, especially when I offer to continue the individual sessions. When I feel ready to invite the patient into one of my groups, the patient is also ready to accept my invitation. Somebody may need a good mother or a strong father or a brother he can kill or a sister to love. I make a definite distinction between a patient's unconscious needs and his conscious wishes. The unconscious needs carry more weight. His conscious wishes are registered and considered but are not guiding me in the choice of the right group. All this is done with an open mind, tentatively, patiently, and without much pressure; thus we have time to analyze the resistance against joining the therapeutic family.

I always quietly assume that I will finally get my way; the patient will accept the group and even the group I have in mind. With several groups available, everybody finds the right group.

FROM A BEGINNING GROUP

The following session was the third meeting of a new group. None of the six participants had known each other before. All were familiar with individual psychotherapy.

The participants were Mark, a therapist; Tom, a late dropout from life; Mae, a depressed playgirl; Ernie, a lost soul at the end of his rope after five years of analysis; Liza, the gentle wife of a cold and compulsive lawyer; and Annie, the sad beauty of the group.

There had been some subgrouping; the "two men," Tom and Ernie, kept together and so did the "two girls," Mae and Annie. Liza remained alone as the only married woman, while Mark, the therapist, kept himself in isolation. Nobody seemed to trust him; everybody pictured him as an observer and not as a bona fide group member.

The hour started with my announcement that the next time I would introduce another therapist as a member of the group. He was in a depression after a tragedy in his family. The group moaned slightly, as expected, and somebody said what everybody felt: "Another therapist?" But when they heard about the tragedy they did not object further.

During the first forty-five minutes there was slow movement almost exclusively directed toward me whom everybody knew through their initial interviews. I grew restless and I felt with growing tension that this was not how the group should proceed. So I turned to Mae who seemed to be near tears. She had given up one boy friend and had started a new relationship with another but was still mourning about the loss of the man she had really loved for two years. The group reacted with silent sympathy to her story.

Knowing that this new group was heavily relying on my initiative, I turned to Annie and asked her how she felt. This was, however, obvious in her face. She had hated herself all her life and felt that she had never lived up to the expectations of her parents in contrast to her sister, four years younger, who was everything she was supposed to be. Only in her analysis had she learned how to accept herself a little better, but still she felt inadequate and almost unacceptable. One of the men joined me and asked her whether she knew how attractive and good looking she was. With a shy smile, she responded that she only recently had accepted that as a fact. With a little more material about her early childhood, it was possible to give her one of those interpretations which I like to give in the beginning of the group's existence in order to introduce psychodynamic reasoning into the group interaction as a special form of human understanding.

I said that her sister had been asked by her parents directly or indirectly to become what she is—namely, a girl and then a married woman. "Now she has presented your parents with grandchildren and everything is harmonious. You have been expected from early childhood to be more than just a girl, and you have tried through all your young life to realize your parents' hopes and ambitions. You became a career woman and have not married. You have avoided marriage because that would stamp you definitely and forever as a woman. In addition to your beauty you have something very attractive to offer: you offer a silent plea to men to develop a relationship and make you a woman and deliver you from the curse of your parents." In later sessions, she extended her plea to the men of the group, and our acceptance of her as a woman slowly released her from her curse.

After a moment of silence, I turned to Tom who was sitting apathetically in a corner like an unemployed clerk. He denied my diagnosis that he was a dropout from life and described himself as more like somebody "on strike." He was not satisfied with his work and did not see any reason to live like a slave. He neglected his profession, postponed decisions, and delayed procedures. At home he gladly worked in the garden, fixed the house, and helped neighbors. That's what he would really like to do. He told his wife that it is now time for her to get back to work after twenty years of taking care of the family. To his surprise she joyfully accepted this assignment and returned to her old job as a nurse. Tom hoped that soon he could close his office for good. I was quite worried about the intensity and determination of this man's regression into infantile symbiosis with a good nursing mother. He managed to become simultaneously nursing mother and baby of the group.

The group was startled by this man who denied his entire life work. I responded to them with an interpretative description, comparing Tom to an infant confidently and quietly sitting and waiting for mother to return. He is not depressed but quietly optimistic that the golden nipple will appear over the horizon and fill the whole sky and his hunger. Then I compared Tom to the quiet Ernie who had been disappointed by his insane mother and his absent father and had had no real points of orientation or identification in his childhood. By being denied nourishment, he had been prematurely catapulted into maturity and gone on the search for a new and good mother. However, he had been severely handicapped in his search for this mother because he always had to look back and see what was happening to his two younger brothers. He was so concerned about them that he never really dared to reach out for his own rights. He always made sure that the two younger brothers were taken care of first, as I knew from my years of acquaintance with them. The two brothers have bypassed him by now and he has withdrawn almost like Tom. He is not as righteous in his resignation as Tom and fears being an inadequate "Schmoo," as he calls himself.

By now, Mark, a therapist by profession, was getting restless. He made some uniquely inappropriate interpretation of his own. Tom and Ernie jumped on him for playing the therapist instead of being just another member of the group. Mark responded by loudly attacking almost everybody but me.

I complimented Mark for the free expression of his aggressiveness during the first hour. He had attacked people he had never seen before and thus had started action and interaction in the group. Even if I did not agree with him, I had to admit he had brought the group to life. I compared him to Tom who had tried to be a good, nursing mother to all, while he, Mark, in his attempt to relate, had defended himself against any affection or pleading for affection with loud pseudohostility.

In my remarks I had mistakenly called Tom "Mark," which Mark picked up with the delight of the psychiatrist hunting for clues. This was my opportunity to demonstrate free-associative response,

which I consider the most important and essential part of the therapeutic process in groups. After a short moment of silence I said: "I did
not want to say only that Tom shows a strong identification with a
good mother and her nursing baby and has already become a good
mother to the group. He is also fighting for all of his sons, including
you, Mark."

I did not at that moment explain that the group had interacted
only with me during our meeting; that would sound like criticism and
criticism alone rarely leads anywhere. There was more I did not want
to say but which I had to now in order to explain my calling Tom by
the wrong name. "Tom is my secret cotherapist at this moment; he
represents my younger brother who was named Mark. He was the one
who remained in Germany and was killed. We were good friends and
he was a good man. I feel guilty about his death even though I spent a
lot of time trying to rescue him, as I am now trying to get you both
started again in life here."

It was then time for the group to finish for the day. We had
started the group at ten to four, and now it was ten to six, which is as
long as I wish to conduct any regular session.

To my surprise, Ernie expressed appreciation for a psychiatrist
who seems human and becomes a member of the group-family. Mae
declared she felt halfway out of her depression. This group experience
was something she truly needed. Annie made a move as if she wanted
to kiss me goodbye, then thought better of it and left smiling.

During the session I had turned to Liza once with the words: "I
don't want to seem to call on everybody in turn because that would be
misleading as if everybody had to wait for his turn." However, she had
said so little and everybody was there to learn how to express himself
spontaneously, freely and honestly. Liza said how closely she had
followed the proceedings and how difficult it was for her to break in.
She then turned away from the group and discussed her home situation
exclusively with me. The change to the better at home was due to the
new attitude she had developed after the last group session. She no
longer waited for her husband to change but started to show him what
she wanted from him.

STARTING THE GROUP AFTER A VACATION

After an interruption, it is more difficult to start a group than an
individual. It is difficult to say goodbye to my families when I go on

vacation, and it is difficult to get things started again when I return – to get six or seven groups to start relating. We all develop our cultural resistance during such intermissions. We submit to social rules, taboos, and manners which are supposed to safeguard against frustration but which actually just substitute good manners for hostility. Although truly free communication and spontaneous interaction do not have to be learned anew, they have to be reactivated after dormancy.

I arrange it so that patients ready to terminate can use our summer vacation as a kind of "terminal leave," as we used to call it in the Army. Then they and we make the final decision after the vacation. I always prefer to do it this way; often, however, the patients say a definite goodbye during the last session before the vacation. I also postpone acceptance of new members during the last two months before the summer vacation and invite new members to join the group in the fall when I return.

I talk so unembarrassedly about such a long summer vacation because it is more than just a vacation: it is a purposeful interruption aimed at the internalization of the group process by the individual. What a person has learned in the group process, he may now apply to himself and to his communication with his unconscious and with some person in his environment, for instance, his marriage partner.

I agree with Franz Alexander (1946) that fractionalized treatment supports the therapeutic process and continues it. When my patients then come back in the fall, they begin usually by comparing notes about their experiences away from the group.

As the hourly sessions have a definite rhythm of starting, progress, and termination, so also the life of the group has a definite annual cycle – a new reconstruction in the fall, progress during the winter and deep into summer, and a kind of termination before the summer vacation.

FIVE GROUPS IN THEIR FIRST SESSION AFTER A THREE-MONTH SUMMER INTERRUPTION

In September 1972, after a three-month interruption, the group of analysts reassembled without any difficulty. June had terminated because she had moved out of town and Bob had not yet returned from his vacation. The rest of the members spent much of their first reunion reporting about their adventures, and I about my fairy-tale existence in the north. During the last half-hour of the session, the problems and conflicts emerged and we knew that we had started.

The Tuesday at five o'clock group collapsed completely. Only one member appeared to announce his determination to discontinue and then there was no more group. I had vaguely expected this to happen, but I was surprised that not everybody was back at least to say goodbye. One member had already resigned from the group shortly before the vacation because none of us had thought him ready for a second marriage and he had felt misunderstood, rejected, frustrated, rebellious. His "sister," as the group had nicknamed a girl in the group with a similar background to his, appeared a week later, and requested to be transferred into another group. Erik decided to continue his work with me in a couples group since he thought that it was now time to involve his wife in further treatment. Two of the women had already said goodbye before the vacation. They had attended the group for several years, and we all agreed that they did not need further treatment at the present time. An eventual return in the future was always left open to them. This was the only time in my experience that an entire group sank under my feet like a ship.

The newest member of this group, who had joined only three months before the vacation, was invited by me to discontinue, since I had the definite impression that his wife had made his attendance in our group a condition of her not leaving him and not dissolving their marriage. I told him that he should postpone his return to the group until he felt a stronger motivation than this once-a-week report to his parole board, as it were.

There is one particular form of resistance often overlooked. Perhaps it is a specialty of mine to react to it. I consider it a resistance when group communication does not move freely but focusses upon one member and stays there. I frequently take the liberty of saying, "I have had enough of this now. Let us change to somebody or to something else." If there is a psychiatrist or psychiatric social worker in the group he or she will immediately raise a voice in protest. Nevertheless, I consider it important that the group should move continuously and at least attempt to involve all members. Procrastination is not a sign of free, spontaneous interaction.

Work on the resistance is the central part of the therapeutic process. The therapist in a one-on-one situation works on the resistance of an individual to communicating with his unconscious, while with the group he works on the resistance to communicating freely with each other. The therapist does his job when he follows one of James Anthony's ground rules: the therapist takes care of the group, and the group will take care of its members.

The group which met on Wednesday at eleven o'clock started with only one half present and the other half calling to announce that they would return to the group a week later. Only one member could not be reached. He too appeared a week later and the group was back to full strength. I do not mind starting with a small group which then doubles its size in the second week. The three people present during the first meeting proceeded to work well, mostly reporting what had happened while we had not met. Starting only half a group necessitates some repetition of stories to members who return later. This is not a loss since repetitions are often a part of working through. Each time the understanding and insights are deepened.

Big Bill told about his deepening awareness of his relationship with his wife and about his love for her. Both of them are surprised about this development. At the same time, however, both are equally afraid of intimate relationships and therefore are careful with each other and cautiously watch their new intimacy. It was clear what had to be worked on during the coming months, and it was equally clear how his courage to love again had directly developed out of his group-relatedness.

Judy and Carol worked well, especially Carol who again had felt tempted to discontinue, feeling alienated from the group because she was the youngest. At the end of the first period she was deeply involved with using the group as a kind of narcissistic mirror experience.

The Wednesday afternoon group was one of two groups which had continued to meet regularly during the entire summer vacation. Franklin was made a kind of spokesman who had the assignment of communicating the group's critique: I had interfered with the spontaneous and free expression of feelings and thoughts during the sessions. Some felt overpowered and awed by my presence, authority, reputation, and by a certain Prussian overbearing.

I reacted to this criticism not defensively, but by explaining it was up to the group to deal with my authoritative behavior, as they called it. I did not promise to change, though I would keep their words in mind. I considered the problem the group's, not necessarily mine.

Everybody then corrected Franklin's statement; nobody really wanted to identify with his announcement. Nevertheless, I had heard what was said and knew there was a rebellion brewing. Part of the group's complaint was justified, and I work on the reason for their complaints as I work on my accent—with remarkably little success. Another part of the complaint involved important group dynamics which soon became obvious: There was a European woman in this group who really came to life only when I was not present. I reminded her shockingly and frighteningly of her father. During the leaderless vacation sessions, all the members had become freer in their interaction and now felt closer to each other. This remained so from then on.

The European woman never returned to her previous, frightened transference reaction toward me. There is no doubt in my mind that her opportunity to talk with the group about her feelings toward me while I was absent helped her to develop the courage to deal with me in the resumed sessions. This then encouraged everybody to be more free and critical toward me.

The Thursday morning group appeared with only one couple missing who were still on vacation. Of the people present only Mark really worked; the others started with reports about their vacation. Rose felt sick and lay down on the couch, a rare occurrence in my groups. Sylvia brought her little baby, born during the vacation, because she was still nursing. This lovely arrangement did not work well, and mother and child disappeared into the waiting room.

By the end of the session a connection to the unresolved problems of before the vacation was established, and again it was clear that we all would continue.

The group which worked best on return was the Thursday afternoon group. I was surprised by the spirit of this group since I had considered it before the vacation as my problem group. They had now turned into a cohesive working group.

This group had met regularly without ever having everybody present. They had always met in a park and the atmosphere was like a picnic. I realized that for one member it had been of paramount importance to keep the group together under all circumstances. This woman's driving need for the family not to break up was related to a strong separation anxiety and was furthermore motivated by her strong competition with me. Martha needed to show that she could be as "good a mother" as any therapist. She had been joined by another woman with a similarly strong wish. Peculiarly enough, one younger woman who had shown an intense anxiety about interrupting the group and who had been quite active in arranging the vacation meetings had never shown up. The story of her behavior during the vacation played an important part in her future analysis of her attitude toward the group and of her separation anxiety.

The three men of the group reported briefly their reality situation during these three months. Otto discussed his deepening relationship with a friend. John talked about his liberation from his depression, which was now a matter of the past. And Alex spoke about the death anxiety activated by his father's terminal illness.

It seemed to me that the two groups who continued their meetings during the summer vacation started easier and better than the groups who had lost contact with each other during this time. This observation changed my attitude toward groups' continuing meetings while I was not present from strict neutrality to slight encouragement. I remain, however, in the background since it really must be the wish of the group and not my recommendation which keeps things moving during my absence. It seems to me that such arrangements are successful only when at least one member is especially motivated to continue, usually as a result of his separation anxiety.

A few years later, I noticed that the need to get together in the summer disappeared from my groups, and everybody accepted the interruption with equanimity.

THE LIMITED VALUE OF ANECDOTES

Occasionally somebody tries to start a group by telling an anecdote. Usually the speaker starts with a sentence like: "Something interesting happened to me yesterday." Then he tells a short story where, as a rule, he has no other function than that of witness and reporter. Here again I do not care to invoke restrictions by saying: "Anecdotes don't lead anywhere. Why don't you say directly what you have to say?" Instead I treat the story like a symbolic communication. In this way it may become significant and meaningful.

Although the events are real, their value lies in their symbolic meaning. The words "on the way to the group" or "to the office" almost invariably lead to a cloaked announcement about the speaker's transference feelings.

Once a member returned from a long, life-endangering sickness which had us all worried. He had reported about it in previous sessions and we had listened mostly with deeply felt sympathy. What else could the group do? At the beginning of this meeting the man said, "Something peculiar happened yesterday. My two dogs, a mother and grown son, were playing when the son yelped in pain having broken his leg. He was treated and must be kept almost motionless in a small space, since he should not run. He wanted to get to his mother, and the mother wanted to get to him, and it was pitiful to watch them."

The story of the young dog with his broken leg not being able to play with his mother, and of his master helplessly staying by was a symbolic description of how the patient himself felt after his operation and in relationship to us.

At another session, Andrew reported in all its details a terrifying incident which had occurred after he left the group a week ago. A truck driver had parked immediately in front of his car and he had blown his horn to warn the driver not to back into him. Thereupon the driver became enraged and threatened violence. Andrew drove off in a hurry. The truck followed him in wild pursuit. At the next red light, they both had to stop and the truck driver got out and challenged Andrew to fight. When Andrew saw the size of the man, he wisely declined the invitation. Thereupon the truck driver attacked Andrew's car in a wild fury. Then the light turned to green, and Andrew escaped, shattered but unhurt.

The story was told as if to illustrate what could happen in the streets of any city, and everybody had to accept the incident as illustrative of the reality we live in. However, knowing Andrew and his central anxiety, this anecdote could be analyzed as if it had been a nightmare of his. The behavior of the truck driver expressed exactly what Andrew thought about his own unconscious: it was full of unmanageable hostility and fury, violence and rage; it had to be repressed at almost all costs.

THE MEANING OF GOSSIP

Once in a while, especially at the beginning of a session, somebody quickly tells or wants to check on some rumors or gossip he has heard. Some members will always protest: "We are disgusted, we don't want to listen to gossip, instead of working." Here in Hollywood, we are suspicious of gossip as publicity stunts or as attempts to ruin a person's reputation. However, it is also possible to analyze gossip almost like a dream, as is done with anecdotes. It often seems to me that there is a nucleus of truth or a symbolic truth hidden in many rumors. A person can dress up a fantasy of his own in the fabric of gossip about others. When somebody questioningly announces, "I hear the death of our colleague was a suicide," then the chances are that the speaker's suicidal or murderous fantasies are being testingly offered in this way.

Sexual gossip is frequently fantasy; for instance, somebody may say: "Hansel and Gretel are being divorced because of a boy friend – not hers, his." Associations may lead from there to the homosexual anxiety or temptation of the one who repeats the rumor and takes delight in talking about it. This of course can be used as a part of the analytic process.

WHISPERING AND SOME OTHER ANNOYING HABITS

Minor annoyances are caused by people who need to be educated before they fit into an analytic group. The first among these are the "whisperers." It is a cheap trick to lower one's voice so as to be heard better and to command the silence and attention of the group. I am too old to hear whisperers clearly, and since my hearing is the foundation of communication and understanding, it is hard for me to tolerate behavior which amounts to a sabotage of the group process. There are habitual whisperers, whom I ask to speak louder, and there are occasional whisperers, who try to draw their neighbor into a subgroup through whispered communication. It is rare that such communication is worth repeating so that the entire group can hear it, but remarks should be heard by the entire group or not at all.

The second group of annoying people are those who abuse and

pervert the process of verbal communication with compulsive, perfectionistic, argumentative indulgence. One of the worst habits is to say: "Define your terms!" We do not define any terms. We expect that our partners in the process of communication listen willingly and try to understand what is said. A definition is required mostly in order to doubt it, debate it, and take it apart to win an argument, not to gain insight.

I am skeptical about any fanatics in the group. People have to be educated to that open-minded tolerance which is the basis of any analytic communication. Fanatics have a "closed mind." This occasionally brings me difficulties with my liberal friends. No matter how good the cause I do not permit collections of money or signatures during the session. It gives a purpose to the group process which is alien to its nature.

People who come late annoy me. Since I have to express my annoyance to the people who are present I may miss the offender or have to interrupt the interaction to talk to the latecomer when he finally arrives. I sometimes threaten to lock the doors fifteen minutes after we have started. As always, somebody in the group cannot stand to participate in a "lockout" and will open the door with my silent consent. I have found that latecoming should be analyzed after it has been criticized or stopped. I am aware that this approach does not look analytic, but seems to belong to preparation for analytic work. I interfere, however, only with a form of communication inappropriate for the group. I do not interfere with the motives which have to be analyzed.

There are a few personal annoyances which I hesitate to mention here. For instance, there is the case of the ill-dressed woman. I want people to dress when they come to the session according to their own taste, as freely, as uniquely, in as much and as little as they wish. I accept gladly the liberal style of Southern California attire which fits the beach and is frequently seen on the streets and in offices of the city. There are, however, women who offend me by neglecting their appearance. Here I do not wait for analytic understanding but go into action immediately. "If you dress this way you cannot accept yourself, and how then should we accept you?"

Some liberated woman once objected to my behavior and asked pointedly: "What about ill-dressed men?" I confessed, to my own surprise, that I had never known or noticed an ill-dressed man. Men may annoy me in different ways, for example, ill-mannered behavior. I do not easily tolerate gum chewing, coffee drinking, smoking, or late arrival to the sessions. I hope I do not give the impression that I create the atmosphere of a penal institution, but I do express myself directly and unmistakably.

The last group who annoy me more than they should are slow payers. I have learned to take it as a warning sign people are considering dropping out and want to combine their exit with a financial advantage. It annoys me greatly to stand before the group repeatedly and defend the economic side of my profession. I do this but with some impatience and anger.

THE NEED FOR GIMMICKS

Frequently in a beginning group, before group cohesion has been established and before confidence toward the analytic process takes hold, somebody will suggest a nude marathon or a swinging party, or he has seen a television show with certain exercises performed with great emotional impact. We finally end up in a discussion of the primal cry or the latest fashion.

I never have seen the need for the use of any gimmicks, as I call them. I never have needed them so far and I do not see why I should experiment with them now. I have usually left the decision to the patients when they have wanted an additional group experience. Any member of any one of my groups may go to any weekend encounter and return to us and report about it. Neither patients nor therapists nor colleagues with whom I have discussed many of these new variations of group technique have convinced me that there is something which could be used to accelerate my analytic approach. I am afraid that the use of any gimmick gives the patient the feeling that it is up to me to come up with some new idea or trick and that he has only to wait for the performing therapist to arrange his participation in the group process. I want cooperation from the beginning, not the expectation of a rape of the unconscious.

All gimmicks contradict the basic rule of psychoanalytic group psychotherapy which is to establish a free and responsive communication and a free interaction. All gimmicks are devices which are planned. This means they are not spontaneous. I proceed without them: I do not paint, either with my fingers or with brushes, I do not ask anybody to get undressed nor do I do so myself. We do not touch each other and we do not fall forward, backward, or sideways. Group psychotherapy is an art in itself and should not be diluted.

I feel as if I am conducting an orchestra when working with groups. I do not run a playground or a kindergarten, nor do I play musical chairs. At certain occasions I may be a performer, but I am never an actor. For technical reasons I may choose to display emotions. However, I honestly feel such emotions; I never pretend. This would pervert the group process.

The only art form which I allow myself concerns language as the art of communication. At times I may express myself with symbols and I may even try to talk in the language of the primary process. I may call somebody, "the eater of filth" or "the fiddler on the roof" or "the unsinkable Molly Brown." I may talk about an "anal Narcissus" or "an anal King Midas," who turns nothing into gold, but everything into feces. There will be somebody who deserves to be diagnosed as "Mother Portnoy." I also may quote from the Bible or from Martin Luther, because their metaphors and symbols reach deeply into everybody's unconscious.

It is my habit to see the work of artists or performers with whom I have to deal therapeutically. I also read the literary products my writer-patients show me. I do that because it gives me a chance to join them in their fantasies and dreams. However, this is not an essential part of communication in groups; it is done more for my information and my knowledge.

A TYPICAL MISTAKE: QUESTIONING EACH OTHER

It is surprising how little has been written about the analyst's questioning his patients, even if it is only with a "Hmmm?" This sound is a question meaning what are you thinking? I am listening and hear nothing.

There is only a handful of questions which must be asked in the group. It is quite natural to ask a newcomer during his first session as an expression of welcome and curiosity: "Why are you here? What do you expect to accomplish? How can we help you?" The reaction to this question is often significant and may predict the course of the newcomer's behavior and the group's response for weeks to come. When somebody is obviously in trouble the group will turn to him either silently or outspokenly with a question: "What is the matter?" To do otherwise is not to be human.

Most other questions are unnecessary or outright misleading.

The worst kind of questioning is what I call the "FBI method of investigation." It is a kind of analytic fishing expedition in which the one who asks the question tries to obtain evidence for an interpretation or response he has already performed in his mind. Lawyers are inclined to bring their aggressive cross-examination into the group and have to be weaned from that habit. People often need to be restrained in the beginning of a group in order to see that their own response is always better than a pseudointerpretation confirmed by questioning.

Questions may be answered, sometimes even honestly, but any answer to a direct question is a kind of closure which stands in the way of the unfolding free-associative interaction.

Questions can be used easily as resistance to avoid interaction, emotion, and intimacy, or to express or avoid hostility. I had to especially be on guard against this habit in a group of senior psychiatrists who went on such fishing expeditions with a passion in order to confirm hunches they had and which they wanted to keep for later use, as they would with a patient. I often set a counterexample by giving my interpretative response to a patient first and then waiting for affirmation, denial, or correction by the patient. I may wait for spontaneously given clues, but I rarely fish for evidence by questioning. This is the reason why I prefer not to describe my practice as an interpretation but prefer to use the term spontaneous response.

Similar behavior is of course frequent among nonprofessionals. For instance, the wife of an attorney had learned from her husband at home how to conduct formidable interrogations. Instead of revealing the emotion felt within herself, she wanted to have the facts clearly before her before she ventured an opinion.

The change from questioning to response is of fundamental importance in the conduct of analytic group psychotherapy.

There is always somebody who will follow my advice to respond and not to question and who then promptly proceeds to develop a new form of resistance. He shoots interpretations from the hip like a cowboy in a movie. He shoots on sight and listens only afterwards to what he has been saying. Such behavior is truly dangerous to the group process and has to be interpreted as a form of resistance and hostility. It is an avoidance of sincerity, honesty, and human responsiveness. Nobody need wait until he can give a well-formulated, clearly thought-out response but everybody must wait until he feels sincerely that what he is going to say is honestly felt.

THE THERAPIST'S ATTITUDE IN A BEGINNING GROUP

There are certain behavior patterns in beginning groups which I simply stop. It is my impression that my interference saves time and avoids possible traumatization of the group members, thus safe-guarding the development of the analytic group process. If someone tries to hold the floor longer than his story justifies and in this way bores everybody, I do not wait for the group to cry out in despair. It is not fair to expect such courage from the group in the early stages. It is up to me to be the model of directness.

I am not a "teacher of life" as psychiatrists are called in Soviet Russia. If I am teaching anything, I am guiding the group in the direction of free and honest communication. The work to establish such communication in groups is the equivalent of that on the resistance in individual psychoanalysis.

INDIVIDUAL INTERVIEWS DURING THE TIME OF BEGINNING GROUP WORK

When I invite a reluctant patient to join one of my groups, I offer to see him individually as long as he thinks necessary. My schedule is so arranged that I can keep my promise. Later when patients are well rooted in their groups, I still grant everybody the right to ask for an individual interview. When an individual in crisis needs more time than he can expect to claim for himself in the group, then he should do some additional analytic work with me. I have found that this privilege is never abused as a form of resistance to work in the group. On the contrary, I am surprised how quickly patients take to the group and let their interviews with me lapse. Patients later are outspoken in their preference for more frequent or prolonged group sessions rather than a return to private interviews. Former analytic patients are especially outspoken – analysts included. There is something about group work which seems to make the working through easier than in a continuous analytic effort. The back and forth of work and rest, the rhythm of group sessions, seems to be different from the persistent slow analytic penetration.

Occasionally I suggest an individual interview myself because I feel the working alliance weakening. I may also realize I am not familiar enough with the patient's history and want to check my knowledge. This has happened mostly with patients who have come initially for group psychotherapy and with whom I have spent probably only one or two hours of preliminary contact. Recently I try to keep such problems within the group. After all, whatever I want to know the group wants to know too and whatever disturbs one relationship in the group, disturbs others.

Here is an example:

John had been in a depression for several months. He always wanted to impress us how deeply depressed he felt, how inefficient he was in his work, how he was sitting over his papers in his office doing nothing, how impossible it was for him even to speak, how much his income had dropped, how he neglected his wife, how he never wanted to go home, never felt understood, how nobody seemed to listen to him.

I realized that I did not understand what he was complaining about and that I was not in touch with him and the reasons for his depression. In this way his complaint had some justification. Therefore, I offered him an individual interview which he accepted with resignation.

During this consultation, I realized that I had actually accepted this patient for group therapy while he was still in treatment with a colleague and friend of mine. I was not, therefore, as acquainted with his past as I usually am. I had had only a minimum of perhaps one hour with him plus a short talk with the referring colleague before accepting him in one of my groups.

During this interview it became clear to me that his depression had slowly started and then quickly deepened after the birth of his second son, approximately twelve months after the birth of his first son. He did not make this connection which became clear to me when he repeatedly referred to July as the beginning of his depression.

When he spoke about his childhood he talked about early primal scene material, about his inefficient father, and about how he, John, had had to bring his mother to a mental institution because of insanity. He was then only fourteen years old. John had been an only child for a long time, working hard on the farm. After his mother delivered twins, she had developed a postpartum depression.

The dynamics of John's depression became slowly clear: the central trauma had been the dethroning of the only son by his mother's pregnancy with twin brothers, mother's psychotic depression after the delivery of the twins, and her final hospitalization–all without the help of the ineffective father, or so it seemed to the patient in his recollection. The trauma of his childhood was repeated in his present situation by his wife's two pregnancies in quick succession and the delivery of a second son, almost a twin brother to the first born, complicating the home situation endlessly. The father, in this case me, again had been ineffective.

The interview was of spectacular therapeutic impact, and the patient walked out of his depression within days, partly as a result of insight into his identification with the mother which was combined with the wish to "undo" her breakdown. Where the mother had failed the patient doubted that he could win. In the transference the "ineffective father" came through with understanding and help.

An unsophisticated, not so young woman described obviously hysterical trembling spells which occurred occasionally when she drove her car on the freeway. She had to pull off the road and wait until she had quieted down. She had no insight into the causes of her anxiety. I was not familiar enough with her and her past to have more than a vague guess as to what the reasons for her hysterical behavior could be. She was so inhibited and so unfamiliar with psychological thinking that her limited associations were of little help. The group suspected that she must have been angry at something and that was where we had to stop.

When I saw her alone the woman poured out a bitter, angry, loud rush of accusations about her husband who had left her, her children who abused her, her boss who disrespected her, her father who was not there when he was needed, her lover who was stingy and selfish, and the group which did not understand her. When she was driving to visit her father she was overcome by her helpless rage and the fear of what would happen if she would allow herself to show her rage. Not even in the freedom of the group could she express her rage; she had to try it first with me. After this interview the patient was able to feel her anger almost instantly. The group could work better with an angry woman instead of a trembling rabbit.

Gisela's central complaint was the feeling of being torn by great doubts about her men friends for as long as she had an affair with one. She felt her love only after she had broken off a relationship, and then she found herself in deep despair. She finally decided to marry, went on a honeymoon, and had a marvelous, happy time. Returning home the old doubts began and she was again torn by envy for anybody else she suspected of having a happier and more exciting marriage than hers. I felt that I could not give her the time in the group she needed to feel understood and invited her to a "marginal" interview.

In this interview my impression was confirmed and I saw now clearly that her fear of commitment was not directed toward her friends as she wanted us to believe, but toward being a woman, or in her language, "nothing but a woman."

She had never felt accepted as a girl. When her sister succeeded in a career usually reserved for men, Gisela felt an intense envy. She was furious at being condemned to be "just a woman" and to become "just a housewife." She did not trust her ability to live like a woman. She could not hate the man she felt she ought to be. When she had succeeded in destroying a relationship and symbolically castrated the man who had loved her, then she collapsed in regret, remorse, and loneliness as though she had also castrated herself. Commitment to a man in love meant to her acceptance of being "just a woman."

There was some change in her toward her sisters in the group whom she recognized as substitutes for her envied real sister. Her envy toward them eased, and she was accepted by the group when she felt that we wanted her to be what she was made to be, namely a woman. The process of working through got a decisive enforcement, and she continued her work in the group more efficiently. The group's message was: we want you to be a woman, equal to the best, and not second to anybody. This message had great therapeutic impact. A few marginal interviews gave me the kind of genetic understanding which guides me in treatment. The final outcome of years of individual treatment, followed by some more years of group work, was nevertheless unsatisfactory. A life-destroying envy seems to be a tough therapeutic assignment.

ANALYZING RESISTANCE IN MARGINAL INTERVIEWS

A man who usually worked well in the group was rather silent and said that one of his obsessions had come back, and he just could not make himself talk about it. We would have to wait until he felt ready. The group did not like this but could not put pressure on him, and the discussion moved on.

At the end of the session while everybody was still in sight, I turned to the man and asked him whether he would want to have a private session with me to see if we could analyze his resistance against letting us know about his obsession. He accepted the invitation.

Alone with me he told me that he felt he had made good progress in the group, in relationship with his wife, and in his work; he felt that he became a much freer man. Many things which were left unfinished in his previous analysis now became clearer to him and could be applied and integrated. However, recently an old obsession had returned: when he looked at his three-year-old daughter, he felt impelled to have sexual thoughts about her. This was terribly upsetting. He was totally unconvincing and did not seem upset at all. Soon it became clear that he was using this obsessive thought to put up roadblocks to further progress. With these obsessions, he could hardly be expected to have decent human affection for anybody. He had similar ideas about somebody else in his family. I told him my impression, and he reacted with a flood of associations which had been effectively blocked.

This man's resistance had not been group-directed, but had been inner-directed against inadmissible thoughts. When occasionally such obsessive thoughts occurred to him later he would ask himself what kind of thought was screened out through his obsessive roadblock.

This interpretation of his obsessive blocking had to be repeated in the group. My knowledge of him from this interview was then quite helpful. At one point in the group process, he suddenly had to confess obscene fantasies about all the women in the room. Without further help he got hold of his associations behind the fantasies–his crying need for love and affection and his inability to admit to his needs. To be obscene was easier to him than to be loving.

Now, several years later, I could and would handle the situation without actively inviting the patient into an individual session. I have gained more freedom to turn my attention from the entire group to one individual patient during the group session. At the beginning of my group work, I had to separate these two attitudes. I learned this lesson observing a colleague in his work. Every time he felt that he had become too deeply involved, he left the room and watched the group through a one-way screen from the outside. This gave him enough distance as an observer, separated him from participation, and freed him for analytic understanding. He then returned with new insights to the group. This external change allowed him to shift from participant back to observer. Watching this interesting procedure gave me the courage to change my attitude temporarily from being group directed to being individual directed.

TRESPASSING THE LINE OF DEMARCATION BETWEEN INDIVIDUAL AND GROUP SESSIONS

When I worked with families, I felt uneasy when I had to protect a family secret until I found out that most family secrets are known by everyone in the family. The taboo of silence is not directed against knowing the secret but against its open discussion. It is naturally not the assignment of a therapist to be the one who violates the taboo and overrules the conspiracy of silence by openly discussing whatever has not been said. It is a matter of his skill, style, and knowledge in working on the resistance first; then the discussion of the avoided topic will follow.

Anybody who conducts individual interviews with members of a group will find himself in possession of privileged knowledge which the individual has communicated to the therapist but not yet to the group. Here again it is not the therapist's assignment to betray the confidence of the patient. His assignment is to lead the patient to freer communication with the rest of the group.

In one of my groups, a young woman had just broken away from a proverbial domineering mother who had almost ruined the health of her daughter. The daughter had gone through a period of demonstrative disobedience, culminating in delinquency and promiscuity. When the intensity of her acting out lessened, she married, became pregnant, and resisted all temptation to reestablish a dependency upon her mother. Since a reasonable attitude was not possible between mother and daughter, the distance between the two women got greater, and the patient continued to mature. Symbolically speaking, the group had invited the patient to bury her mother and to accept the group as a better mother.

Occasionally the patient confessed some of her obsessive thoughts. These decreased slowly in intensity and occurred less frequently, finally moving far into the background. She revealed once that she had one fantasy which she could tell only to the analyst personally but which she was too embarrassed and ashamed to reveal in the group. She fantasied that she enjoyed sex in the presence of her mother, and only this made orgasmic pleasure possible. To tell the fantasy in the group, she had felt, would destroy her ability to reach full orgasmic satisfaction ever again. Her anxiety could be interpreted that to talk about her fantasy and reveal her sexuality in front of the group mother would lead her immediately to uncontrollable sexual excitement.

A VISITOR TO THE GROUP

A young man was visiting a group in which his wife was a member. We all felt the need to see him in order to compare the impression gained from the stories told by his wife with our impression of him when we saw him. The young wife had always shown great tact, understanding, and even tolerance toward a man for whom none of us felt much sympathy. The stories about her home life, which could have been devastatingly told, were reported with a sense of humor worthy of James Thurber.

It had been the feeling of the group that nobody could live with such a man and that he should return to therapy, which he had left after using his superior skill as a manipulator of men to defeat his previous analyst. The group did not want to be a jury with me as judge; we wanted to understand the difficult situation.

The husband acted immediately at home in a group of people he had never seen and viciously and coldly began an accusation of his wife. She watched him silently, neither intimidated nor annoyed but with thrilled expectation like a spider waiting for a fly.

The group reacted to the man: "You behave like Portnoy in prison, expecting your wife to liberate you. Your wife cannot liberate you since it is safer and more important for you to accuse than to love. You fear love as if it were the original sin."

It is a matter of opinion whether such a group response is a valid interpretation or just a metaphoric explanation. The effectiveness of the interpretation depends upon the work done after it is given. It could grow and become a basic, deeply felt interpretation, or it could remain just another unremembered remark.

In this case, interpretation was not even directed toward the visiting husband but toward his wife. Our message to her was that nobody can put up with such behavior and save his sanity and self-respect. The consensus of the group was that the man was worse than his wife had described him.

TRESPASSING THE TABOO AGAINST TALKING BEHIND SOMEBODY'S BACK

During somebody's absence from the group for whatever reason, good or bad, I always probe the group's feeling about the absent member. It is my impression that it is not natural when the group does not react to the absence. Occasionally in beginning groups, I may even volunteer my own feelings first. I set the example for breaking the taboo of not talking behind somebody's back. I may worry about somebody and fear he may have experimented with heavy drugs again, or that somebody else may have gotten into trouble because of his driving, he may even have been arrested. I may complain about the absent member, "He has not worked recently with us," or "He was withdrawn," or "We must confront him with his attitude," or words to that effect. Almost unfailingly somebody will say: "Let's not talk about anybody who is not here." I make it a point that we should talk not only about our relations to the absent member but about the fact of the absence and our feelings about it. Whatever we say now behind his back will be repeated in different form when he returns. Breaking the taboo is an exercise in courage.

AN UNUSUALLY SLOW STARTING GROUP

Sometimes it takes a long time before a group has reached an analytic level of free associative communication and develops spontaneous, responsive interaction. It is a question of the therapist's patience, intuition, knowledge, style, and feeling for the group. One group started to move only after great initial difficulties.

While the group was assembling in the office, Rose tried to isolate me from the group by taking me aside to explain something quite banal to me. Then she wanted to use the telephone to call home. She did this in front of the entire group, disregarding the interruption which her behavior caused. I could see how the group was building up a hostile reaction to this, our newest member.

When the group began, Karla told a dream. Shortly after that I asked about something I really wanted to know about: how was Gustave's wife feeling after her pregnancy since she had left the group? And had her anxiety returned? After her husband told us, I retreated into silence while one after another, the group stepped forward to report about progress or lack of it. No interaction developed spontaneously.

Although I do not like to berate any group for not working, I said halfway through the session: "What is the matter with all of us? Why don't we have a group today? Everybody is on his own; everybody talks to me as if we were alone."

My answer to myself was: "I, and probably the group, feel annoyed at Rose and nobody has the courage to say so. I repeated and described her behavior at the last session when she had been looking at a book and had only put it away when I had asked her to do so. She had responded joyfully that she could do two or three things at the same time. Today she had been trying to isolate me from the group at the beginning and then used the telephone and annoyed everybody. I confessed my hesitation to talk about these things since I did not want her to say, "Once a Prussian, always a Prussian. Why don't you go back where you came from?"

My remarks were like throwing a lighted match into dry brush. The whole group now criticized Rose's impertinent behavior. Although she was new, she had become a prominent group member; she had already arranged social events and had visited in almost everybody's house. She was well liked and highly respected as an unusually gifted young woman. However, her tactless use of her position as the favorite and privileged child of the group provoked an outburst of antagonism now.

By then Rose was in tears and she could neither defend herself nor explain her behavior. An interpretation was offered: "You behaved with childlike charm and innocence as if you wanted to say 'I am a child here and I have certain privileges. You must love me anyhow.' We did and we don't." The incident began the analysis of Rose's provocative exhibitionism.

Soon everybody felt that perhaps Rose had had enough confrontation for one day, and Christopher took over with a vicious attack on the therapist. For once he could cry out against him. He had seen the therapist attacking and slaughtering another member, and he wanted to attack before he was slaughtered as the father's next victim. He had always been a mother's boy without a father. The boy had wanted to be liberated from being his mother's only son. Occasionally, perhaps once or twice a year, the father had reappeared and kindled his son's love, and then after a happy Sunday afternoon or a weekend at the most, he had again disappeared. Nobody knew what was happening to him and whether he was still alive until he again appeared. With his outburst, Christopher defended himself against a repetition of this relation to his father with me.

Originally this group had hesitated to attack a new, annoying, and provoking member. After the therapist set the example for criticism, all hell broke loose and aggression was released which culminated in a confrontation. This led to the beginning of a chain reaction of interaction.

INTRODUCING A NEW MEMBER INTO THE GROUP

I do not ask the group whether or not they will accept a new member. They know that any opening will be promptly filled. However, I do not introduce a new member to a slow-open group without a previous announcement. This gives the group a chance to ventilate their response to a threat of the established pecking order. Some may want another man or another woman, only a young person, or a group-mother, or somebody beautiful. Some prefer larger groups, some may want a smaller one.

If I notice strong opposition to my intention of introducing a new member, I follow the feeling of the group and either give up my wish or delay it until the resistance is understood.

Once I introduced a newcomer by saying something like this: "As you know, we have a vacancy in this group and we should fill it with a woman. I have a woman on my waiting list with whom I have worked a number of months, and I think she needs a group experience now. She is one of the most unrelated young women I have ever seen. She and I have barely formed a workable relationship, and I would now like to try her in this group. She is afraid to join us but has agreed to try it. She is shy, timid and withdrawn, but not to a degree which makes it impossible for her to work. It is possible that she will do in the group what she sometimes does in other social occasions, namely, force herself into active participation. She is driven by fears and anxieties, she has no real feeling for herself and is often plagued by feelings of devastating unworthiness."

After such an introduction, I know what reactions to expect. People will say, "Don't you have somebody else? Somebody who brings some movement into this group?" I would not expect an outspoken opposition; that would contradict the readiness of the group to help. I never ask for a vote, and only in cases of real group rebellion will I say: "If one of us is really against this new person, I will not invite her to join us. However, the final decision is mine."

Another reaction I might expect is, "That's a hell of a way to introduce a newcomer! What did you say about me when you introduced me?" I truthfully recount what I remember having said or ask: "Who remembers what I said?" Repeating the record demonstrates to the patient that he knows what I think about him. It should go without saying that the patient's suspicion of me has to be analyzed too.

In the specific case of this woman, the group experience became a life-changing and life-saving turn for the better. The group accepted her at first with benign indifference during a long period of waiting for her to participate. This group attitude was replaced by a curious turning to her, to which she slowly responded.

Lately I have shortened every introduction of a new member and limit myself to an announcement of his or her first name and those of the group members. The rest will develop without my managing anything. I learned that whatever happens spontaneously in a group is preferable to any arrangement.

ANALYSIS OF A THREAT TO INTERACTION

During the following session, Benvenuto was missing from a group of eight because he had to attend some business out of town.

I felt highly annoyed because a veteran of the group, who should have known better, had called shortly before the session and brusquely announced that he could not continue to come for financial reasons. I reacted to him over the telephone with anger and wanted the group to know about it. I had said, "This is a silly reason. You know very well that these few dollars make absolutely no difference to a man who has a palatial home, a second beach house, and runs a business undisputed in our part of the country." He had to agree but insisted that he had to stop. I responded that he was of course the master of his decision, but would he please have the courage and decency to come to the group and say so himself because a one-sided decision is just not possible in a group? He would have to make his announcement here to us so that we could react to it and change the ties which everyone had developed to everyone else, especially to him who had attended the group longer than anybody else. He did not respond to that and said goodbye, whereupon I, and I am embarrassed to confess so, said brusquely, "Go to Hell!" (which certainly is not an expression recommended in any therapy). It had, however, the result that he appeared on time.

In my annoyance, I opened by asking Rita why she had neglected to dress well recently. She explained that when she had been very unhappy she had lived for the group and thought about it throughout the week and dressed for it like for a feast. Now that she is happy, she remembers the group at the last moment.

Then the would-be deserter, Carl, took the floor and, as often before in previous hours, he held the floor, almost desperately, hoping somehow to get to the point. For once we all were listening, nobody lost interest, nobody was aware of the long time he needed to say, "I am afraid to be thrown out of this group, and I prefer to go voluntarily. Sarah never liked me, she despised me and I despise her whispering about me to the other people during the group when we leave. Big Bill has the typical snobbishness and arrogance of a prominent man, and he will never accept me. Rita is in love with somebody else; she hardly sees me. And Carol has all the arrogance of youth and is not interested in anything else but herself and the therapist. Grotjahn annoys me terribly because of the difference between our individual sessions where he treats me decently and the group sessions where he steps on me as if I were the crumb of the earth, joining in the antagonism which has developed between the group and me."

I responded to that by saying: "You want to be accepted as a shitty baby and this is asking too much from the group. We do not want to accept you on that basis. We want you to grow up and be a member of the family, not to be a dirty, perverted, sneering little brat. The change in your attitude to the group happened when you felt embarrassed about the confessions you had made here. At first you tried to play the role of the goody-goody baby which was as equally unbecoming to you as the role of the shitty baby. You behave to us as you did to your mother who was supposed to love you no matter how naughty you were." I added some illustrating evidence from his previous responses.

Myron reacted to Carl with annoyance as I did, and with astounding understanding. "Today you have talked straight for the first time. I never heard you, and I never talked to you. I hardly ever looked into your eyes. Today I did. You have trusted us and now we will listen and trust you. This will help you to feel acceptable and not to insist on your masochistic and exhibitionistic provocation. I have lived for sixty years without ever having felt accepted by my mother or in my profession or in the circles in which I move. Neither have I ever believed that my analyst thought of me as a worthwhile person. This group accepted me and I have accepted the group. This is the greatest experience which I have ever had in my years of therapy or in all my life. I always felt like an outsider. Here I am on the way to becoming an insider, and here you and I meet."

The rest of the group reacted in a similar way, even if nobody could match Myron's warmth and affectionate understanding. Carl remained silent and thoughtful. This was a turning point for him.

THE GROUP'S RESPONSE TO NEWCOMERS

After the nuclear group of four or five people has been more or less established and has developed a sort of group cohesion and begun to interact, I invite more members until we reach at most eight members. This procedure is the easiest for the group, the newcomer, and the therapist.

A new member always offers stimulation, sometimes a challenge, and rarely a threat. Mostly he stimulates new interaction. Frequently changes in the pecking order are required.

The group gains new insight from dealing with the new arrival and the newcomer himself experiences his first encounter with the group's response to him. This is occasionally painful but mostly therapeutic and rarely traumatic. It sometimes takes the entire skill of the therapist to negotiate between the newcomer and the group in order to avoid traumatization of an experience which should be therapeutic. Later when the newcomer has found his place in the group family the intensity of the responsive interaction changes but remains of central importance. Several examples of such responsiveness have been cited here already.

When I talk about "good groups," I am thinking of groups where the participants have learned how to respond spontaneously and not superficially and to trust their feeling without becoming impulse-driven. A group member who develops this courage and freedom will be able to handle any situation in or out of the group. The aim is to learn how to develop this kind of free communication with others and with his unconscious. The free and spontaneous communication corresponds to the individual's work in analysis when he learns how to communicate with himself and his unconscious without anxiety or guilt.

I consider the experience of being a newcomer of such importance that sometimes I recommend moving somebody to another group in order to allow him a second confrontation with another group. My wish is often firmly and consistently opposed by the patient invited to change. It always amazes me how strong the feeling of group cohesion, loyalty, and bonding is among group members. It is always a good lesson for the therapist to realize that the group members do not just come to see him and to hear his words of wisdom, but that they rely equally strongly on the group.

The variations of the group's emotional reactions to the newcomer are so numerous that they cannot all be described here. I must also confess that I have not mastered the art of introducing a new member without slowing the group process temporarily. This delay is usually limited to the first session or a part of it. At first the group, which had been informed at a previous session that I will invite a new member, will try to proceed as usual by ignoring him. He is considered a witness until somebody asks: "What do you want? What do you hope to gain from us? What is wrong with you? Why are you here?"

AN EMBARRASSED RESPONSE TO A NEWCOMER

Once I introduced a new member to a group of seven people who had worked well together, especially during the previous three months. Four weeks before, I had introduced a new person, now to be followed by a second new arrival. It was kind of a dramatic beginning. Someone reported to the group about an adventurous experience of his which simply had to be told to the group. After this topic had been discussed by everybody, one of those hours developed in which everybody stepped forward and reported on his progress or experience of the week and very little interaction developed. A therapist reported about his schizophrenic patients who drove him out of his mind with frustration. Somebody else spoke about his visit to his son, and one of the women was deeply depressed about having heard that a friend of hers had died. Everybody presented his complaint or worry and illustrated it with a story without being aware that he was presenting himself to the new member.

I interpreted the group's behavior as a way of introducing themselves to the newcomer who was a tall, impressive looking, elegant, young woman. From the little I had announced about her the previous hour, it was known to everybody that she was extraordinarily gifted and successful in her career. Everybody wanted to present himself in an interesting light. They were all slightly embarrassed about the newcomer who behaved like a silent observer. Somebody finally asked her what she expected from the group. The new person lived up to the situation and gave a short and pertinent summary of her situation and the group was off to a delayed start with fast-moving interaction.

The group had been split in its wish to welcome this unusual girl, and they expressed this wish by introducing themselves with illustrative stories. Simultaneously there was considerable antagonism toward the girl, as if they wanted to say: "What do we need her for? We were a good group before with a nice flexible hierarchy and now everything is upset again."

The newcomer herself mastered the situation smoothly, stating her problem as she saw it, and she soon became an accepted member of this group.

OTHER VARIATIONS OF RESPONSIVE INTERACTION

A group had discussed whether they wanted to accept a new and especially beautiful woman as I had suggested. All the men were enthusiastic about it while the only woman in the group was indecisive and agreed with the group's acceptance only after some hesitation. The predominantly male population of this group was the reason I wanted to have this new woman join us.

When Jenifer appeared for the first time a week later, she was painfully shy, timid, and inhibited. She did not know where to sit, fearing that she might take somebody's accustomed seat. Finally, she sat next to the door as if to secure a quick retreat. After a few minutes, she curled up and sat in the corner of the couch waiting with intense interest but looking terror stricken. Everybody in the group was fully aware of her discomfort; some shy attempts were made to make her feel more comfortable and to show her that we welcomed her. Then everybody picked up where we had interrupted a week ago, and Jenifer was almost forgotten.

The man to her right later moved his chair closer to her and smiled at her with genuine paternal affection. Later he said that he felt toward her as if he had found a new daughter. After the session Jenifer was so terrified that she asked for permission to remain seated for a few moments in order to avoid any kind of contact with the members after they left.

During the next session a week later somebody turned to her and asked: "Why are you here? What do you expect?" And Jenifer answered with great honesty: "I do not like myself. I do not even like to think of myself. That's why I don't know myself. I do not know who I am. I feel myself only when I am working. I have Satan in me." This she said peculiarly soberly, and it had a pronounced effect on us. Eve, the only other woman in the group, turned to Jenifer, wanting to put her at ease, and invited her to go to lunch with her afterwards so that she could tell her a little about the people in the group and the way we work. Eve remembered how she, a woman with great social poise and experience in the world of men, had also been frightened to death the first time she had attended this group.

With real shock Jenifer answered: "Oh no, don't underestimate me. I can take care of myself." She visibly took all her courage and proceeded to explain why she was here. Her previous analytic experience did not count because she and her analyst "were not on speaking terms." She felt already now, the second time with the group, as if she were among friends. She already felt no longer outside of the group but had confidence and felt free to talk with us.

She expressed her feeling of being at home with the group, in the way she was dressed. The first time she was dressed in a red T-shirt and a black velvet full length skirt. This time she arrived with her hair unkempt, flying all over her face and back, a blouse with buttons missing and with the dirtiest blue jeans ever seen in my office. We were supposed to accept her anyway, which we did.

The men of the group reacted to her confession of confusion, self-hatred and shyness by showing her how they felt. Mike told her the story of his life and was in tears as he talked about the lack of closeness through all his life, which he felt must have been somewhat similar to her life. Richard talked about his physical sickness and his envy of athletic men.

It just so happened that this was the week before the Easter holidays. We were a small group, and a deeply felt intimacy had sprung up among us. The fright and loneliness of this little girl symbolized the terror of loneliness in us all. Our acceptance made her feel that she finally had found what she was looking for—a family of friends who understood her and would not hurt her. She had arrived home, as it were. Her acceptance was only a beginning, but a good beginning, and her group experience was to influence her greatly in times to come.

THE GREATEST MISTAKE

The greatest mistake a newcomer can make is to claim that he is here to learn and to study the group process. This is always greeted with loud indignation.

Roberta had been asked in her first session why she was here and she answered that a friend of hers was in another group of mine and he was so enthusiastic about it that she thought she should come too, especially since she was working as a school counselor. She would like to see how group work is done. The group reacted instantly with threats to throw her out. "We don't need another psychiatrist; we don't need an observer. Our family is not for visitors; this is not a show." She was considered haughty, and cold. Roberta retreated in bewildered pain, not knowing what she had done to deserve such a reception.

Soon she discarded her pretense of professional benefit and accepted her position in the group as just one of the family. She was accepted by us, with some reservations. Our original first impression of her aloofness and haughtiness was nevertheless correct. She wanted us to believe that she was strong, self-sufficient, and independent–a model young woman of our times. It took some time to show her that she too was human and a woman. This insight was painful, but was soothed by the group's message: "That is the way you are and should be, and we love you for it. You will be a better counselor when you accept it."

7

The Group in Progress

This is the place to repeat that it is not my ambition to describe in detail the technique of conducting group therapy. I want to give an impression of how *I* conduct analytic group therapy, and how I handle transference, resistance, interpretation, responsiveness, and interaction in my daily work with groups. I will demonstrate the unfolding of the group process with some clinical examples.

James Anthony, who spent a lifetime with analytic group therapy, said, "To take care of the group is the assignment of the therapist, then the group will take care of its members." This more or less is the guiding line of my approach.

There is something else which I have learned from James Anthony: the group is not fragile and the analyst working with groups can proceed by allowing himself at times a technique which would endanger the analytic process in the one-to-one relationship.

The following pages collect loosely arranged clinical observations covering and illustrating the main events in groups after they have started and formed a cohesive group—a firm matrix, bound by the multiple transference. It takes approximately nine months of work for a group to reach the degree of free communication, interaction, and responsiveness described in this chapter.

THE USE OF DREAMS IN ANALYTIC GROUPS

The place of dreams, their analysis and their interpretation in analytic groups, illustrates most clearly the difference between individual analysis and analytic group work. I spent forty years in psychoanalytic work. I use this experience now to interpret dreams reported in the group. The members in the group, and I, respond to the dreams with our associations and emotions. The group response takes the place of interpretation. It also could be said that the response is the interpretation or carries it. The group does not wait for detailed or confirming associations as it is done while analyzing an individual. This is like the direct or wild approach sometimes recommended in the treatment of psychoses. The dream of one member of a working group becomes the dream of all members, their common property, a "Dream of the Group."

Here are some examples of the place of dreams and the depth of their possible interpretation in group work.

Several members of one of my groups had seen, independently of one another, a movie in which a woman loved a young man, who in turn was loved simultaneously by a middle-aged physician. The young man oscillated freely and seemingly guiltlessly between his male and female lovers.

The oldest member of the group hesitatingly reported that as far as he was concerned his homosexual conflicts had been solved many years ago, and the movie had left him cold and finally bored him; if he had not been with friends he would have left. At this point one could feel the reaction of the entire group that the man was in a resistance. Without being interrupted the speaker continued: "To my surprise I had a nightmare in the middle of the night after having seen the movie. I dreamed that I was sleeping in my bed; it was total darkness. I was aware of a powerful young man who tried to get on top of me, to roll on me and to squeeze me or to choke me to death with his weight. I was frightened for my life and tried to prevent the man from killing me. In the struggle, I awoke and realized that I had sprung out of bed and across a low table, sweeping it clean of books and pencils and papers."

Now everybody was ready with the interpretation of latent homosexuality activated by the movie. The dreamer listened quietly

and remarked that he had thought about all of this. Then he volun-
teered a few associations. The young man was a composite of his tall,
strong son; his younger brother, now dead; and the young assistant
who helps him in his work. From there his associations moved to a
movie he had seen three years ago in which a middle-aged woman
allowed herself a last fling at life. The leading female figure was
followed everywhere by a silent, motionless young man who followed her like a shadow and obviously represented death.

From then on the associations in the group vascillated among all
the members talking about well-controlled latent homosexual trends,
their affection for each other, the freedom they had achieved in this
relationship, their happiness and their disappointments in their children, and finally they talked about the serious illness of one group
member who was absent. As we approached the discussion of death,
the session was ending. It was not clear whether the theme of the
session had been homosexuality or death, or both.

At the next meeting the man who had reported the nightmare
had a new dream which he said made "absolutely no sense." The
dream was unusual for this group since most dreams reported here
were already predigested in that the dreamer has tried to analyze them
before reporting. The speaker had dreamed that he was a student and
back in the auditorium of a university. It was a small class with only
four or five people. He was listening to a young instructor who gave
karate lessons. The instructor called each student out in front of the
class and showed him how to fight, ending each demonstration with a
blow effectively showing his students who was the master. "When
my turn came, I was aware of the difference in age between the young
instructor and me. I was aware that he was vastly superior to me as he
had shown in his fight with the other, younger students. I was calm
and confident. I quietly reached for a cookie cutter with which I
proceeded swiftly to cut the instructor to pieces. I awakened with the
feeling of the cookie cutter in my hand."

It now became clear that the speaker was concerned with problems of aging, dying, and being replaced by younger men. When his
time to die came the young men would continue to live. Consciously
he accepted this, but unconsciously he was fighting it with murderous
rage. The murder instrument used points to an oral cannibalistic
introjection of the love object, and that is where the roots of homosexuality may be found.

ANOTHER DREAM

The hour was slow moving, perhaps because it was the last session of the year and everybody seemed to feel as if it were the last day in school before the vacation and that the teacher should tell stories, which, however, he did not do.

A woman of thirty-five, in her first marriage and pregnant for the first time, started to tell a dream. "I was giving a big party. Some women made snide remarks and I threw a number of them out." The group's response was immediate and unanimous: the big party symbolized our group sessions, which according to the dreamer had "too many other women." They compete and represent bad mothers and bad sisters and they should go home and never be seen again. She may as well be the only woman here. Altogether little was said since this interpretation was so obvious.

The speaker continued with another dream. "We wanted to buy a new house. We found just the right one, but there was no room for entertaining. I was heartbroken. All of a sudden I recognized that there was such a room. It was perfect and in all its details exactly as I wanted it. It was amazing that I had not known it." Her associations went to her husband who was also a member of the group. A dialogue developed between the two with the group witnessing it. The problem was her coolness and his sensitivity. He complained that she was only rarely turned on by him, and she complained that he was never satisfied.

As so often in groups, the dream was obvious to everybody but the dreamer. She had discovered that she could enjoy sex to the fullest, at least occasionally, and lately more and more frequently. She had discovered "a new room" in her body which she was getting ready for a "party," meaning for sexual pleasure. The new discovery of the room in the dream also represented the baby to come, which now filled space in her body she had never known to exist.

Christopher responded by remembering dreams that he had a few days ago. "My mother wanted me to type something for her. I was in a terrible rush and told her so. I didn't want to do it. But I quickly typed it. In my hurry I mistyped the word *Hollywood,* and it came out *Horrowood.*"

By telling it, the meaning of the dream became clear even to him. His mother had always been a "horror" to him, and she had spoiled and finally wrecked his first marriage. He was now, many years later, getting married once again, hoping to have delegated the image of the bad mother into the past.

DREAMS EVERYBODY UNDERSTANDS EXCEPT THE DREAMER

A woman had interrupted her participation in the group because of a severe sickness which necessitated hospitalization, major surgery, and afterwards complicated treatment. She was greeted with sympathy and warmth when she returned. She participated little and remained silently observing.

When she began to feel at home again in her group-family she told a dream: "I was embraced by an octopus from the back with tentacles reaching around my body. But it was not really an octopus, it was hairy. I loosened the grip of the arms and this hairy thing let me go. I turned around and I saw it running off, it joined its own kind, a group of its friends."

The patient was frightened by this dream. She had not felt horror, only a feeling of uncanniness. Only now telling the dream, she felt the full impact of the small but horrible monster.

There was no doubt in any one of the group that the woman had dreamed of her sickness, a tumor, and her wish to be liberated from it and to see the tumor go where it belonged, into the museum of pathological specimens. After the interpretation, the dreamer was annoyed that she had not understood so simple a dream. The interpretation of the dream is in itself no answer to anything. To find and understand its meaning is like opening the door to a room. How to deal with the symbolized problem – that is the assignment of the working through process in analytic groups.

DREAMS ABOUT THE GROUP

John was dissatisfied with himself, the group, the therapist, his wife; nothing was right. He had started group therapy when his wife had threatened to leave him because she found him too cold, unapproachable, obsessive, and uncommunicative – an unfeeling robot. The group had shown him how to live differently. He had tried it, had allowed himself to get in contact with his feelings, with his great inner rage, and with his need for intimacy. Now he felt open to being hurt and as far as he could judge, everything had become worse.

Here are his two dreams from the night before this group session:

"A group of attendants was working on my car and I had great doubts whether they could do the work right. They waved me off with the words: 'We know what we are doing.'

"Later a doctor gave me a physical examination and asked me to swallow a fish line with a hook which would make it easier to examine my throat. I had great doubt that this would help and feared that it would damage me severely."

It was clear to everybody, perhaps even to the dreamer, that the inept garagemen represented the group and that the physician who demanded poor John to swallow something "hook, line and sinker" was the therapist.

A DREAM NOBODY UNDERSTOOD

At another group session, almost without any introduction, John told another dream. A big hunk of meat was hidden under his bed. Rats were eating it and when he looked closer he did not see rats but maggots. Soon the meat looked half eaten and turned into the body of a woman and he woke up.

The dream did not speak to anybody. There was a moment of silent contemplation and when John refused to offer any association nobody offered any response and the group turned to other topics and somebody else took over.

Almost at the end of the session, I returned to John's dream. I had interviewed him a few days before, alone without the group. He had told me in this interview about his childhood. When he was a boy of ten or twelve, his mother had delivered twins and afterwards taken sick with a severe and ever-deepening depression, leading to years of hospitalization. While telling this story, he recognized the similarity between this tragedy and his present situation. At the time of his mother's hospitalization, which overshadowed his youth, he had to take the place of the mother in the family and had to take care of the father and the two little twin brothers. At present his wife had delivered a second son only one year after the delivery of the first one and he felt that the two boys were "almost twins."

When he saw the similarity between his past and his present and his identification with the mother and all the difficulties of having to care for twins, he was able to work his way out of his depression within weeks. Having now seen therapy at work, he sent his wife in order to safeguard her against an eventual depression.

Now the dream became clear. It seemed to symbolize the return of the insane and long-dead mother, in the form of the body under the bed, to haunt him with the threat of mental sickness.

After this interpretation he associated primal scene material. He thought for a long time about the bloody murder his father had been guilty of by fathering twins and driving his mother into insanity. He felt guilty now for many reasons, but especially for having risked his wife's life and health by giving birth twice in such a short interval. At a later time, the hostility against the two little brothers and his sons could be faced more clearly.

THE INROAD OF REALITY: THE DEATH OF MARTIN LUTHER KING

Almost at the end of the evening session, shortly before seven o'clock, the telephone in my office rang. It could be heard that it was the emergency line, which had never before interrupted a session. I made a remark of apology and alarm to the group and lifted the receiver while everybody fell silent. The voice of my wife could be heard through the room saying: "They shot Martin Luther King! And it is not known how serious it is. They interrupted the broadcasting to bring this bulletin—" There was a pause of silence and then my wife continued in shocked sadness, "Yes, they killed him."

In such a situation, it is natural and the only thing to do to stop everything and either to watch for further news together or to disperse so that everyone may go to his own television set and join the nation and the people of the world in grief.

There was little said about this experience in the next group meeting a week later. It seemed, however, to me, that the group had made another step toward closer cohesion.

Less tragic and less dramatic events can break into the group process at other occasions and must be handled differently, as the next example may illustrate.

THE HANDLING OF POLITICAL CONTROVERSY

A middle-aged man had complained about the behavior of his son who had joined the rebellious opposition to the establishment. The father said that his son had been arrested by the "pigs." I was shocked that an adult would use such a term to characterize a fellow man. Some of the group were nonplussed and others seemed to agree, but half of us thought that this term was inappropriate and that it was horrible to call anybody such a name. The dialogue turned into a heated political debate. There was the danger that the group would spend the session in a political argument. Until then, politics had been mentioned only briefly from time to time.

It would be wrong to stop a debate with an authoritative restraint such as "We are not here to debate the war, the admission of China into the United Nations, or any other political issues." To stop the group process in this way would be against the principle of unlimited free-associative communication. At the same time there is no doubt in my mind that this kind of argumentative discussion does not belong in any analytic group. I consider such arguments as resistance against the true purpose of the group. It is, however, not enough to diagnose the resistance and let it go at that. An interpretation of the resistance must be offered. As a rule this can be done only after the discussion has been started and is on its way. If the debate is interrupted too early a bad precedent has been established. Politics are an essential part of our reality and cannot simply be excluded from the microcosmos of group work.

In the case of the "pigs," I had a chance to interpret the father's behavior. First, I made my stand clear that such words are inexcusable. Policemen are people too and our brothers. Then I showed that the father had joined the son's rebellion against the establishment. He was quietly feeding the spirit of revolt to his son who took to it with a passion, got into serious trouble, and had to pay the price for his father's rebellion. The issue of the hour was to understand the acting out of the father through his son and to show him how he simultaneously enjoys it vicariously and complains about it.

In political debates, I always state clearly my position in case there should be any doubt in anybody's mind about where I stand. Only then do I try to break through the resistance into the psychoanalytic aspects of the debate.

THE ANALYTIC NOSEDIVE FROM OUTER TO INNER REALITY

One somewhat unusual group session started with a general and easy discussion of one member's wedding reception, which almost the entire group had attended. One member, Mark, apologized for not having been present because he had been just too busy with his deteriorating family affairs and his imminent divorce. His reasoning sounded convincing but was interpreted by the therapist differently: "You had to face the failure of your marriage, your failure as a father, and your financial difficulties. You did not need to be reminded of your misery when a friend got started in a new marriage." Mark defended himself, claiming that he had really wanted to come.

From there I went into some interpretative remarks about everybody's behavior at the party which I too had attended. The woman who was being married had played marvelously the great, good nursing mother to everybody. Dick was his sweet self, enjoying himself greatly. Bob seemed to have felt guilty about being there and Mike had felt terribly out of place. The group responded to my remarks: "And you were the analytic observer as you always and everywhere seem to be. You don't live, man!"

I had talked this way because I did not want to avoid talking about the reception; that would have been contrary to the principle of free associative discussion. I tried to use the group's common reality-experience, which had taken place outside my office as a starting point of interpretation. My commentary on everybody's behavior was intended to highlight the psychological side of the event and offer it for discussion. It proved successful as we now discussed the psychology and not the reality of the event.

I then turned to Mae, the other member of the group who had missed the reception. I had offered to take her to the party with my wife, since I knew that she would be sitting at home alone on a Sunday afternoon, not daring to move. As predicted, she called at the last minute and explained that she had another very important engagement and could not possibly make it. My unusual offer was made, as I now explained to the group, in order to show Mae that I can easily and happily live in two different worlds. At my home I live like a student in an ivory tower, but every once in a while I can join the world of reality and enjoy it without trouble, embarrassment or conflict. This does not need to cause anxiety and fear and does not need to be avoided. One should master such situations and such shifts from one life style to another. Mae avoided such changes because of her anxiety and stayed home in bitter withdrawal and isolation.

I did not wish to show myself as a shining example or as a model of how to live. I wanted to illustrate an alternative life style for Mae to consider. The invitation was also an invitation to join this, our group family. She reacted with anxiety, and it took a long time for her to believe we really meant it when we reached out for her.

This incident illustrates what I call "the analytic nosedive" from the external to the internal reality. It was possible to move from the recounting of a real experience to an interpretation of behavior.

Before the group was fully assembled, Karla loudly and bitterly burst out that she and her husband had invested all their money in a new business venture of Gustave's, another member of this group. Gustave had promised to double or triple their investment and now found himself unable to repay the money and had asked for another extension of the loan. They were worried beyond words. When Gustave arrived a few minutes later, he listened calmly. It was immediately clear to him what we were talking about. He had a hurt expression but didn't seem worried. I was worried about this turn which I had not expected. I did not know that any members of the group were engaged in financial deals with other members.

By then Tom, Karla's husband, could not control his anxiety any more and asked for his money back. He was impatient, tense, and hostile. Gustave simply stated that he could not and would not repay him for a while. Tom yelled: "What am I to do now? Get an attorney?" I did not have an answer either, so I waited.

By now the whole group was in an uproar, everybody was ready with advice, everybody asked for more information, including Vivian who had joined the group only a week ago. I wondered whether I should have cautioned against financial arrangements between members of the same group. These people had been friends and neighbors for many years before they had come together as a group to me. I felt concern about the group's future, in that reality problems might crowd out analytic contemplation.

I remained silent and waited for clues to go below the surface. Tom's disappointment and Karla's anxiety about possibly losing their money seemed disproportionate. I could not resist a slight feeling of triumph seeing greed frustrated. I was slightly alarmed when Rose loudly declared that Gustave's behavior had been "unethical." Before I could correct this term, Gustave angrily said: "If Tom really wants his money back, he will have it tomorrow. But it would be inconvenient and it would delay and endanger the future growth of the project." I began to worry less about the reality.

Karla listened to her husband's anxious complaint and found an opening for an analytic understanding which surprised me since she was definitely ahead of me. She said: "Once more Tom has to face a terrible disappointment in his father, and he is more upset about that than the possible loss of money. Tom was disappointed by his father, his professors, his beloved previous therapist, and now by this 'sugar daddy.' Grotjahn should have warned his children about such dangers." Tom responded by relating additional events which had recently activated his persecution anxieties. A neighbor had started a lawsuit against him, and it seemed that everybody was out to get him. With that the entire group began to talk about parents who disappoint the hope and expectation of their children.

This session significantly illustrates "analysis by the group." While I was still waiting to understand the situation, an interpretation was given not by me, but by a member of the group, Karla, who had helped decisively to understand her husband's persecution anxiety.

I learned another lesson – to be most careful about financial arrangements between members of the group. They are potentially more destructive than any other form of acting out.

A SENSE OF CLOSURE

I have a strong sense of closure which prompts me to "keep things moving." When the group concentrates on one member or begins to belabor a point or when the group starts asking too many questions instead of responding, then it seems to me that the focus of the debate is overworked. I follow my wish to close the subject and shift attention to another topic. I leave it to the group to protest and will listen to this protest carefully.

I take it as my right and duty as a conductor of the group to turn the group associations in a different direction. I have been criticized, especially in a group of young psychiatrists, but also in other groups, for "avoiding deep emotion," or for "escaping from one to the other." These are actions for which I do not feel guilty. I always watch the entire group and go there, where I feel we are needed most and where the emotions are.

I had worked with this group in the following session for two years after they had already worked for several years with another therapist who had suddenly died.

Everybody congratulated Mark on becoming the father of a happy and healthy son. He had been present at the delivery. He had had some anxiety about it and neither his wife nor his mother had expected him to stand up to it. When the delivery started he had no anxiety, he performed well and received congratulations from the physician in spite of moments of danger when a Caesarean operation had to be considered and prepared. The only bad moment had been when he told his father about the happy event and the father made some disparaging remark.

Here I had for the first time a sense of closure. I suspected that in this, the first session after the birth of the baby, nothing else would happen beyond the response of the group to the happy event.

So I turned to Tom and asked him how his holidays had been. His wife Karla answered for him: It had been the happiest time they had ever had. Being a passionate writer, she had written it all up as an essay exercise. She had had a dream of spending an entire happy day with me. She remembered that she had been happy with her father in her childhood except for her mother's jealousy and interference.

As on previous occasions, the group responded to Karla's intensive attachment to her father and to father figures in her life, to her first therapist and to her present one. The group felt that Tom treated his wife like a sister and that he offered her to the fathers. He himself wanted to be loved by the father and made a silent bargain: If you love my wife you love me. Karla played her part in this arrangement well.

She maneuvered her husband into the position of a brother who would allow her to flirt with the fathers. There is a secret understanding between the two: Let us play brother and sister to a loving father.

The interaction was not simply between Tom and Karla and myself, but it was with the entire group, especially with Mark, who interpreted my attitude to them. Mark was a specialist in intuitive, perceptive observation and interpretation of my attitude toward the group. The couple's involvement was everybody's conflict – a pleasure and problem with which we began to cope.

After considerable time I had again a sense of closure and wished to go on to some other topic. Tom and I turned simultaneously to Christopher. Tom had spent an evening with him and had been amazed at the happiness between Christopher and his young wife. Both men were married to much younger wives. The group was inclined to doubt Christopher's happiness, but I made the point that we might as well wait until trouble started and not look for it on their honeymoon. At that moment Julie began to talk about her husband who was suspicious and jealous. The situation during the holidays had been complicated by her son who had been doing so well in school but now was on vacation and upset the whole house. A family consultation was arranged in order to deal with that complication as on previous occasions.

This was the point of a fourth closure, less outspoken than the first one. By now we had moved into the last fifteen minutes before time to adjourn. I had turned to Vivian and described her behavior to her. She had joined the group only recently. This group had worked together for several years and had difficulty accepting any new member. Each time she had tried to enter the group, she had been corrected, censored, and rebuffed, whereupon she had withdrawn in tears. Today she was slow moving and careful. Before Vivian and I got into interaction, the group turned to Rose who was sitting in a corner obviously depressed. The group had asked her before what the matter was, and she had said she did not feel like talking. Now at the last minute she told how upsetting her new house was and how she could not do without her husband who was overworking himself in his office. I gave her an interpretation of what a new house meant for a "new woman" who had become a wife, the mother of a baby, and now the owner of a big new house. She had started a new life, symbolized in the new house. Finally I said clearly that I was angry at her and Vivian for starting a highly emotional and important topic when it was practically too late. I did not like them to sit back and wait until especially invited to join us.

The sense of closure during the session had changed to a sense of opening new issues for the next week. We would have to see how we could understand Vivian's fear of joining the group and Rose's reluctance to accept a new chapter in her life. As it turned out, Vivian's ambition was to become the problem child in the group-family, and Rose wanted us to do her work for her.

SYMPTOM RELIEF THROUGH
THE CORRECTIVE
THERAPEUTIC FAMILY EXPERIENCE

Patients may shed bothersome or occasionally painful symptoms long before they understand the meaning of their sickness. This seems to happen more frequently in groups than in analysis. It is as if in analysis the patient expects his analyst or the mysterious analytic process to perform the work. In groups it is obvious from the start, or becomes so very early, that the patient will have to do the work by himself. The symptom may be given up as a kind of present to the entire family.

The most astonishing symptom relief is reached by people who come to the group with sexual disturbances, mostly premature ejaculation in men and frigidity in women. One fifty-year-old man, married and with several grown-up children complained bitterly about partial and later total impotency. The man discussed with the group first the possibility of divorce and then since he did not wish to desert his partner of thirty years whether he should go quietly but determinedly on his own way.

Nothing seemed tempting or even workable until one day fate presented him with a loving, easy going, warm and attractive young woman. The patient continued his work in the group for several years without any complaints about sexual difficulties. It was as if he needed only the permission and encouragement of his group family to start a new life and to unfold and live a life different from the misery of his parents and from his own misery in the past. This man's therapy was more than simply a convenient way out. It was a true change of his person and his outlook on life.

Perhaps it is a sign of our time that sexual disturbances in women also are given up with greater ease and speed than in the past. When a woman complains about lack of sexual satisfaction and when she lets the group know about it, then it can be safely assumed that she is ready to give up her symptom soon. She then hears about the sexual health and sickness of her sisters in the group and she participates in open and frank discussion. She finally begins to live again, as a result of this corrective family experience.

Many forms of sterility in women can be successfully treated in group therapy. All the women who wanted to have children, could not conceive, and were waiting for adoption became pregnant in the first year of group therapy. The group made these women feel feminine and accepted them as women so that they finally accepted being women willingly and often joyfully. I found this observation confirmed by almost every experienced group therapist. The therapeutic family says, "We want you to be a woman, we love you as a woman, you don't need to try to be anything else." Since this carries the full impact of the transference situation and since the message is what they wanted to hear in the first place, it often acts as a deep going corrective family experience.

An attractive, intelligent, gifted girl joined the group because she felt "almost perfect" and wanted to be "perfectly perfect." This word was her favorite expression and she clung to it with determination despite the collectively raised eyebrow. Her narcissism was emphasized by her beauty. She succeeded in antagonizing everybody, at first the women and soon the men. As a rule attractive young women are easily accepted, and I distribute them carefully and evenly among my groups. This girl, however, antagonized everybody.

Once she went on a trip to participate in a nationwide contest which she won. When she returned I was startled at something which I had not noticed before and which began to annoy me–her quivery, almost quaking, childlike voice. It became obvious that her family wanted her, the only child, to remain a pretty little thing–a cute doll. She had learned to become the perfect daughter and had a marvelous relationship with her parents who adored her and she them.

The group did not command or order this woman to change her voice. They noticed it, reacted to it, and imitated it in order to let her look into a voice mirror. Nobody told her to speak differently. The message which she received as loudly and clearly as she had received the message from her parents to remain a little girl was simple and straightforward: "We do not want a little girl with a little voice. We want you to recognize that you are now a grown-up woman and that all this show of the perfect, clean living daughter belongs in the past. You are a wife and a mother and you should talk like one."

The patient got the message and in a few weeks she assumed a new voice much more becoming and appropriate for her age and status in life.

Fate catapulted this young woman into a fantastic opportunity which she accepted calmly as due to her, and she was never seen again. I am afraid she missed her chance to proceed from being a perfect narcissist to becoming less perfect and more human.

RELIEF FROM COMPULSIVE AND OBSESSIVE SYMPTOMS

There is an abundance of case material about the analytic treatment of obsessive and compulsive neurotics. There is hardly any mention of this specific form of neurosis in group treatment. I have seen compulsive and obsessive behavior in several cases and it is always instructive to me to see how well these symptoms are influenced and eased by group therapy.

Alex, a young accountant, started to describe his compulsive thinking in the first hour of his group therapy. Whenever he had to talk to somebody and come close to him he thought compulsively that his breath might harm the other person. He had then to go through a compulsive ritual of undoing. This was especially outspoken in relationship to his newborn son. The obsession was interfering with the natural and spontaneous enjoyment of the baby and he was painfully aware of it.

When he felt exposed to being breathed upon by somebody else then he had to think that he was being greatly harmed and another countermeasure of undoing had to be instituted. He reacted to the group with enthusiasm, warmth, and spontaneous acceptance to which the group reacted in kind. The group responded also with definite worries about the severity of the symptoms and the bizarre nature of some of the rituals.

Within the first three months of his participation, the symptoms disappeared and when asked about it he simply stated: "I willed them away." He had become tired of it, considered it unnecessary, and after years of this torture thought it time to stop and did so. At a later time the symptoms re-appeared in milder form. They finally disappeared for good after he understood the meaning and function of his neurosis.

Another member of another group returned from a visit to his dying brother. He was upset, sad, and torn with thoughts which made him feel disgusted with himself. He thought his brother would be dead soon and the entire family fortune would become the surviving brother's undivided property. It could be shown to him that this feeling was a defense mechanism in order to keep him from a mournful breakdown. He reacted with great relief in better understanding of himself. The prompt loss of symptoms did not interfere with later insight into his hidden hostility toward his sick brother.

In two men, I also observed the slow disappearance of severe highway phobias. Both men had to come a long distance to my office. They had to use the freeway and at one high and elegant curve both men were almost paralyzed by the fear that they would drive off the curve, crash their cars, and die in a ball of fire. Both men had to force themselves not to turn off the freeway, which they occasionally did, and rejoin it at a place less inviting for an acting out of their "self destructive trends," as they called them.

The group listened to the fearful description, and at first did not react to it. However, both men left the group with new insight into their hidden hostility. They recognized themselves as two angry young men. While talking to us, they listened to themselves for once, and became aware of their rage. When we then learned more about their background, we realized that their phobias of highway driving were actually another expression of their constant fight to repress their murderous wishes and to ram their cars like kamikaze pilots into the enemy, dying a hero's death.

There was a time when both men preferred to be driven by another member of the group family whom they joined on the way. Another member was driven by his wife for a while. Later, when the fear of the rage could be analyzed and the hostility worked out, both men could ride along the freeway in relative comfort. One of the men made a peculiar remark later. He kind of missed his phobia. With that remark he confessed that he secretly enjoyed his murderous fantasies against which he defended himself with phobic symptoms. This was the same man who at another point in therapy threatened me in a blind rage.

ON SILENCE

Groups respond to silent members as if they were not carrying their share of responsibility. They are often treated like millstones around the neck of the group. The group can become quite vocal in expressing annoyance, impatience or disgust.

I once had a therapist as a member of a group who talked very little, if at all. He was a born listener. The first attempts to remedy the situation were attempts to understand the reason and the message of his silence. Our understanding may have been correct or incorrect but it was not of much help. If one waits long enough almost everybody finally begins to talk. At first it is usually an attempt to be helpful to an individual. Only later the person with chronic silence may talk about himself. By then the group may have proceeded from annoyance and impatience to indifference and resignation.

Another patient hardly talked at all for almost two years and still the group was not impatient. I did not probe but turned occasionally to her invitingly without getting much of a response in words. The difference between the silent psychiatrist and this silent, sad-eyed, depressed woman lay in the different quality of their silence. The psychiatrist's silence seemed to be hostile, a sign of his indifference and haughty stubbornness. The woman's silence seemed to be a kind of apology as if she were telling the group: "I don't want to burden you with my sorrow, my sadness, and the agony of my life." This included the death of a husband after thirty years of marriage and of her mother – both within weeks of each other. I had told the group about these events and we waited for her.

In my experience it is rare that the entire group falls silent. It sometimes happens that a group is constituted of newcomers without experience in the group process. Before such a group develops, the one who talks feels as if he is losing group status and isolating himself from the rest of the silent group. He may feel like betraying the united front of silent people. It is up to the therapist to break this kind of silence.

In later stages of group development, silence is usually short and one has to develop a certain tolerance for this. Group silence reminds me of the unprogrammed first day meetings of the Quakers where everybody feels comfortable in the silent worship until somebody sees the light and talks, often to be followed again by silence.

The silent patient is different from the mumbler, somebody who speaks with low voice and does not speak clearly enough for me to hear. This annoys me greatly and I say so loudly and without guilt or apology. This is occasionally mistaken as something emerging from my Prussian background into democratic therapy. I do know that resistance cannot be broken by command. Only interpretation helps, which I combine with such a request.

CONFRONTATION OF THE UNCONSCIOUS AS A DEATH EXPERIENCE

It seems that people do not commit suicide as long as they are actively in treatment. They may try and even may succeed when treatment is interrupted or before they can be rooted in a group or in relationship to a therapist.

If I watch depressive people in a group I am always again amazed at the speed at which they take to the group and with which they gain the first relief from their depression. Finding a group family allows them to accept the little love and affection they permit themselves. In their own family, affection and tenderness frighten them; they must reject it because they feel too guilty and too worthless. They maneuver themselves into situations where they lose their love objects; they slide deeper into their loneliness and suicide seems to be the solution.

The group is inclined to accept a depressive patient. The group is also aware of how a depressive member expresses with his depression an often intolerable aggression against his family. Depressive people are hostile people. They cannot master this hostility and feel guilty about it, lonely, and on the way to hell. The group has it much easier since it deals with such hostility with benign indifference.

There is another trend in a group which is felt by depressed people with relief and that is the feeling of getting in contact with other people's troubles, worries, traumas, conflicts, and despair. When they get the message from another member, "Don't bother me, I can't cope," then they feel that they are not the only sad sacks in the world and a part of the deadly loneliness is lifted. They realize that "God is not here either" and that other people have learned to accept that and keep on living anyhow and enjoying this one life which we have. The group is benevolent and indifferent, yet and still an accepting, unobtrusive mother.

Mark had taken a long time to tell us about the turmoil in which he was living. There was trouble with his wife and children and with judges, juries, and attorneys. He usually got the group and me to advise him about what to do first and how to bring order into his reality. His best friend, who had known Mark for many years before they both had joined the group, interrupted us and said sternly, "We are not here to advise Mark how to run his life. We cannot straighten out that mess, but we must analyze him so that he does not maneuver himself into such a mess again."

Mark defended himself lamely, and I half-heartedly joined him since I believe that nobody can be analyzed as long as he lives in such disorder. Nevertheless we all stopped trying to help him in this way.

The discussion then turned to other people and after about half an hour I turned back to Mark, saying, "Only a man with great death anxiety can live in nearly psychotic confusion as you do. You prefer this mess to facing what you have to face. You have re-enacted a bloody mess of a traumatic primal scene." The group was not inclined to follow this topic and nobody would respond to this interpretation.

Later, during the same session, I repeated my remark which slowly began to make sense to the group. A breakthrough of the unconscious is felt like death. A confrontation with disorder, the timelessness and the chaos of the unconscious, is a confrontation with death. It actually is death, a death of the ego which is the only witness of death. Only the ego knows death, the unconscious does not. The primal scene, chaos, the bloody mess, disorder and psychosis are all symbolic representations of death.

"Dealing with death is of great importance for everybody but especially difficult for you with your intensive and murderous hostility toward a brother. You want him to die so that you may live. Your hostility is that of Cain toward Abel. The bloody mess in which you live keeps you in such confusion and madness that you feel everything only vaguely and nothing clearly enough to feel guilty and depressed about it."

It took Mark a long time to understand this – many weeks of progress and many moments of sudden and deep recognition – until he worked his way out of his outer and inner turmoil.

The longer I work in psychotherapy, the more I am convinced that the discussion of death and dying has been neglected.

The group is capable of analyzing the fear of death. Anything concerning death and dying is easier discussed in a group than when two people are alone, as in analysis. In the one-to-one relationship there is always the frightening implication that one of us must die. This leaves little space to move in before the moment of truth can be faced. In a group there is a way out by assuming that everybody must die, not just you or I, but anybody. That makes the discussion easier, if not easy.

When a member of the group dies, something in everybody dies, but the therapeutic process continues. Therapy is not terminated as in analysis and everybody has to deal with the problem of death and dying. Every departure from the group by a patient who either dropped out or graduated is a death symbol and a threat and activates separation anxieties.

The fear of death is the model for all fears. When one member leaves the group, his departure symbolizes death, as in the fantasy of a child – to go away means to die. The whole process of group therapy is symbolically reminiscent of death and rebirth. This symbol is, as far as I can see, more evident in groups than in psychoanalysis.

I watched a patient for many years through his puberty and early adolescence witness the slow death of his paralyzed father. Later his brother got sick with an illness that turned out to be terminal. The patient developed a fear of death and only open and honest discussion in the group liberated him from his anxiety. The fear to die symbolizes often the wish to kill.

"FOR WHOM THE BELL TOLLS": SUICIDE AND THE GUILT OF THE SURVIVORS

The death of a member in a group is the death of something in everybody. The suicide of a group member shocks the group to its foundation.

No therapy reaches sufficient depth as long as the fear of death and dying has not been discussed in detail and analyzed. The life-threatening illness of a group member or a death in somebody's family, a psychotic episode, or a suicidal attempt has to be faced by everybody in the group and cannot be settled by a conversational conspiracy of silence. These are experiences with which the group has to deal almost as if it happened in a family. It must be faced as a reality, as it must be understood as a symbol of all human anxiety.

Dreams of extraordinary beauty point to union with the idolized, loving mother symbolized as Beauty. Death can be seen and experienced as the final embrace with the mother who, as we assume in our unconscious, is faithfully waiting for us in eternity.

Only once in the experience of group psychotherapy did I have an encounter with death. We learned that one member of the group had died in the week between two meetings. The reason was given as coronary occlusion and no suicide note was ever found. My first reaction was outrage. How could this happen? To a man so many years younger than I was? Everybody in the group had to ask himself, "Could I have been of help during the last moments?" The group went through a period of mourning and emerged from this time of stress even more closely knit than before.

To have lost a friend was part of our group experience. To have been faced with the frightful definiteness and reality of death in the midst of life was the other part of the process of working through, and that lasted for many weeks. It was, of course, not the only topic of the group's interaction.

In the years of group work I also had to deal with members who became fatally ill and had to discontinue treatment. When the sickness became known to the group, the sick person as a rule preferred to retreat from the group.

In the face of death none of us knows how to behave. It is, however, our duty not to avoid learning, understanding, or relating to the unavoidable fact that human existence has a definite end as it has a beginning. The entire hierarchy of anxiety and suffering must be dealt with at such times.

ACTING OUT

I often say at the beginning and during the development of a group, that "this is not a psychoanalytic kindergarten. You remain on your own and you are responsible for what you do; you are not dependent on rules or regulations how to behave. I do expect you to remain loyal to the group and not form an alliance which has to be kept secret from the group. Whatever you decide to do outside with one or several members of the group is your responsibility. The main point is that you should not put a seal of secrecy on such arrangements. Everything that happens in relation to the group should become a part of the communication, a part of the group family's property, and of the group-knowledge. Otherwise you destroy group cohesion."

Sexual relations are so casual and happen so naturally nowadays that I do not think it is up to me to set taboos in the conduct of group members, even if I could. I leave this question open in order to set the stage for free communication, whatever form it may take.

Among the instances of sexual acting out in my groups, only once did the man request the woman not to mention to the group what had happened. The results were inhibiting for both participants until the story was told. Then all the material behind this resistive taboo could be discussed and become part of the group's interaction. The only damage resulting from this acting out was a temporary interruption in communication. The man had been badly frightened because he really thought that he had committed a crime: he behaved as if he had stolen a woman from the harem of his father-therapist. Needless to say, the woman, sexually inexperienced as she was, felt as innocent as the freshly driven snow.

Other incidents of similar nature proceeded without any unfavorable impact on the therapeutic process. Occasionally two young people go to bed with the same ease with which they go out to dinner together.

Another couple enjoyed each other's company for a short period of time, talked to the group about it and soon separated from each other as casually as they had started. An experience of love can be of considerable maturing influence on the lives of both participants.

I have found no reason to set sexual taboos or to change my attitude toward analyzing such events as I would any other interaction between group members.

Occasionally I even doubt whether the words "acting out" are correctly used here, although I always recommend keeping the possibility in mind that the members have acted out their unconscious instead of analyzed it. What happened between people may have happened in class, at a party, or at any other social occasion and does not necessarily include the essence of acting out – defiance and rebellion which is oedipal or even pregenital in nature. In other words, not all acting out is antitherapeutic. Any action like any emotion must be considered by its own motives.

I do not believe that even true acting out interferes necessarily with the therapeutic process. I consider it more a dramatization of the unconscious conflict, in most cases in the form of stealing the woman from the group-harem of the therapist-father. When the man wanted to keep his love affair with the woman of the group a secret, then this request was a sure giveaway of what he wanted to hide. It was the crime of Oedipus. The Erynniens of the group would not let him come to rest.

TREATMENT OF THE RICH, THE FAMOUS AND THE BEAUTIFUL

I follow the established tradition in the conduct of groups and use only first names. I am often surprised that even after a group has worked together for several years, the members may not know each other's last names. We don't keep names a secret, we just do not use them.

I am usually addressed initially by my full title and later by my last name. Veterans call me by my first name, which I prefer and which I suggest from the beginning.

Since for me group treatment is primary treatment, it has nothing to do with the financial situation of the patient. I do not suggest standard analytic procedure to a patient just because he can afford to pay for it. I introduce people into the group regardless of their financial status.

Every once in a while it happens that people are introduced into the group whom everybody recognizes by name or reputation or from television. Their situation at the beginning of group interaction is different from that of other group members. This has to be recognized in order to smooth the way for them to become like any other member.

The fact that the group members know such people by name, status, position, or through the movies they have made, or prizes they have won, the gossip which is told about them, the marriages with which they have entertained the public, or indiscretions which have become public knowledge opens the group suddenly to a new aspect of its work. The experienced therapist has learned how to handle these people in therapy, as he has also learned how to relate to them in the group. As always, his own attitude toward them is decisive for the group's behavior.

All through the pages of this book, the message runs that everybody is at times a therapist and sometimes a good one. I furthermore emphasize that the group can be trusted, and that I have never been disappointed in this trust. The group has never betrayed the confidentiality of any big name people. Nobody went home and said "Guess who has joined our group!"

The beautiful people themselves are inclined to be suspicious and paranoid; they need careful preparation and initial protection. The few near indiscretions which have occurred were all committed by the big name people themselves.

All these people are accepted by the group members within a few sessions and treated just like everybody else. At first there is a certain startled reaction. Everybody is self-conscious, the men show themselves from their most favorable side and the women retreat into pleasantly expectant waiting. Then the group's genuine decency takes over and after two weeks everybody is again a representative of himself and the newcomer is accepted as a part of suffering humanity.

To be on show, day and night, on the stage and everywhere may become a great stress; to shed that need to perform and all their pseudo-identities is the first relief these people feel after joining the group. They have to start the search for their own identity and sometimes they have to build one first. Peculiarly enough, this experience makes them also better actors.

One special word should be said about extraordinarily attractive or even beautiful women. I have been blessed by them in my practice and I appreciate their value. They function in a group like flowers in a garden or an object of exquisite art in a room. They are not therapeutic necessities but when one can arrange for their presence the room lightens, the atmosphere is conducive to the search of truth. The men discover the best in themselves and show it; while the women are more slow in their reaction. They observe their beautiful sisters, and then they try to adopt them. To be beautiful has its glory and its despair. An admiring therapist may have lost a part of his efficiency temporarily but a therapist who denies the beauty he sees has lost even more.

It is time to suggest to these frequently narcissistic people that they transfer to group therapy when they are ready to share their therapist, and when the therapist is ready to share his precious patients with the group.

As a rule the trouble does not lie between the well-known person and the group but between one prominent person and another one in the same group. Such confrontation is better avoided or very carefully timed.

If at all possible I try to take well-known people into groups where the majority may have had a chance for previous social contact at parties, committee meetings, or benefit performances. This precaution shortens the duration of the initial startled reaction.

THE MERITS AND THE DANGERS OF LOUD
AND HIGHLY EMOTIONAL CONFRONTATION

Occasionally highly emotional confrontations take place in groups. As a rule I do not tone them down, which could easily be done. I neither avoid them nor do I provoke or arrange them. Only rarely and then only when I am myself annoyed at somebody or something do I participate in such a clash. The sign for my interaction is given when the group process is threatened.

The group gains little from a dramatic display and even less from a vicious argument, conducted to hurt and not to gain insight. A group gains much when somebody makes his feeling for or against somebody known. Arguments lead at best to victory and defeat, and nobody gains anything; confrontations may lead to insight. Dramatic display of a primal cry belongs in the actor's lab, not in the group.

One of my groups contained a woman fifteen years senior to the average age of the group. She appointed herself as cotherapist and soon as supervisory boss. I like to benefit if somebody – and this may or may not be a professional therapist – applies his therapeutic skill well, perhaps in an attempt to compete with me or to help the group process. If a therapist-patient avoids too anxiously being a therapist in his group, he cannot be his true self. He denies identification with the wish to be a healer. A therapist as a patient in a group should neither try to be a therapist nor is he allowed to deny through his behavior that he is one.

I like it when somebody challenges or interprets my behavior or comments on my interaction with others. If done for the purpose of dominance, aggression, and destructiveness, then I see a danger for the group and rise to its defense. Such was the case with this woman who did not let a free dialogue unfold or an interaction take place without interfering with her know-it-all attitude. I called this to her attention and interpreted her behavior in genetic terms. She came from a large family, with a number of brothers and a domineering, dictatorial father. To fight for dominance had been her fight for survival. No interpretation helped and the group grew impatient and later loudly hostile. The group behavior was best summarized by its youngest member who finally cried out: "Oh, fuck off!" The group's hostility found its mark and the patient left the session twice only to be recaptured by the group after the meeting. After some more struggle, she finally found her place in the group-family.

At other times a confrontation may be unavoidable and necessary to save the group and may lead to sad consequences. In one group, a middle-aged woman was proud of her figure and displayed her charms freely. She did that as if to say: If you are a man you must love me. To such a challenge most men react sourly. Two of the men sitting opposite her finally told her to come dressed more decently. She was so enraged that she threatened to resign from the group. I told her that such confrontation is an opportunity which she would not have in any other social situation. Nobody would tell her as frankly and as honestly about the reaction she was causing in other people, as we here. A woman in the group said: "Do you think we would waste our time here to tell you what we think about you if we did not care for you?" Nevertheless, the woman left the group with the words "Who needs this?" and was not seen again. It is possible that she went to another therapist in order to look back at this disastrous experience and then perhaps to learn from it. At least, that is what I hoped she would do.

In another group a man had newly joined and become quickly dissatisfied with the group. He felt that nobody was as intense as he was and he wished to be referred to a group where there were more lively people. I pointed out to him that once in a while a referral to another group is helpful, but I did not see that it would be helpful in his case. I did not consider it possible to find a group of people where all were more to his liking. He might as well try right here to see what was wrong with him.

The group did not like the attack and slowly they reacted quite intensively to his complaint and showed him how shallow his loudness was, how he forced himself, how frantically he was running around and away from the true issues, and how his anxiety would mount when he listened in silence. Again the therapeutic alliance was not strong enough for the confrontation, and he was lost to this group soon thereafter.

Confrontation later during the group work must be handled with as much care as in the beginning. There are definite merits of such stern confrontation and sometimes nothing else promises any help. Confrontation should be a learning and not a traumatic experience. Highly emotional confrontations are of little value in themselves. They cannot be avoided, but they are nothing to be proud of or aim at.

THE PLACE OF MARRIED COUPLES IN GROUPS

Originally I thought that married couples should be treated together in the same group. I have done so but I have changed my attitude lately. I have learned that it is better to split up couples if prolonged group therapy is planned.

At first I realized that partners work better when sitting separately. They do not come to the group in order to sit there and hold hands but to work out their conflicts and problems, their difficulties and their sorrows. This is done better when they confront each other instead of forming a unit which is a symbolic denial of their difficulties.

Then I learned what is generally accepted now, that it is a mistake to have only one married couple in a group of single people. They may form a united front and if either of them is attacked by anybody else from the group, they close ranks and do not act with that degree of spontaneous and frank honesty which is the basis of the analytic group process.

Of late I have placed married couples in separate groups until they have learned to be honest and frank without being destructive to each other. I always plan on taking them together in the same group for the terminal stages of treatment. For some reason that seems never to happen.

A GROUP MEMBER REPORTS ABOUT HIS EXPERIENCE IN A NUDE MARATHON

Benvenito was an outstanding executive, having arrived at the top of his profession. He held a commanding position in the hierarchy of his industry which had given him the behavior and even the looks of a Roman Emperor.

He decided after thirty years of marriage that something was wrong with his entire life and it had to be changed. He went after this new life with all the energy of a general taking over the administration of a newly conquered province. He visited several psychiatrists, sent his family to be interviewed, and finally joined a group. He was arrogant, haughty, and while always insisting that he is just another patient, tried not so subtly to take over and give advice like orders. The response of the group was not too gentle, and he had to learn how to listen which was a new experience.

In the second month of his participation, he reported that he had participated in a nude marathon. Being the man he was, he had participated in two successive marathons, one of six men and two women and one of six men and twelve women. Nobody was obliged to take his clothes off, but on invitation everybody did without hesitation with the exception of the only black woman in the group who remained dressed. He described then how he had felt. All his defenses as a captain of industry were gone. He became just another human being. It felt good while it lasted. He returned to being his highly defensive real self on the way home from the marathon.

While he was talking, he related to us for the first time in a different manner and the group reacted to him with a new rapport. We almost joyfully welcomed him into the community of humans. He had made the first step toward becoming honest to himself and to us.

It was our impression that the nude marathon alone would have left the man practically unmoved or untouched after it was over but the marathon experience was integrated like any other emotional experience through the consistent analytic treatment in our group. This had helped him to keep the lesson learned alive and effective in himself. The nude marathon probably had speeded up his progress. He remained in the group for several years and his interest in more adventurous forms of therapy soon faded, as it usually does.

8

Problems of Termination

The basic rule which guides me in terminating treatment is misleadingly simple. Since the patient took the responsibility of starting treatment, I assume he can also remain in charge of himself and determine when he is ready to leave the group. Naturally, I will have an opinion and will make this clearly known. I rarely invite any patients to leave the group. I will frequently be doubtful about his wish to leave and only when he has convinced the group that it is time do I stop opposing him. I always consider his wish to leave at first as a resistance against further work.

The group never wants to see a member leave, while I am much more open-minded. I may regret that a patient leaves, because he has become an important member of the group-family and still agree that his time to leave may have come.

I do not agree with anybody's wish to leave in the last two months before our traditional three-month summer interruption. I know that I am tempted at that time of year to wish everybody to go and leave me alone. So, I say carefully. "We should make our final decision after we get together again in the fall."

In evaluating the success and failure of treatment, I have an equally simple rule. I am optimistic enough to hope that nobody leaves the group without having achieved some benefit. I am equally pessimistic (or realistic?) enough to know that nobody is cured. Nobody recovers from the shock of having been born. The group can prevent this shock from leading to lifelong invalidism but a scar will nevertheless remain. Perhaps the time will come when some kind of postgraduate, lifelong education, will be part of everybody's life style.

The pain of leaving is not just felt by the patient but equally by the group and to lesser degree by the therapist. I remember one member who after leaving told me, "I miss these two hours a week when I can be honest and frank, without fear and compromise."

It is rare with slow-open groups that an entire group dies or leaves. Sometimes over the years, a group develops such cohesion that nobody leaves for a long time and then all of a sudden everybody feels ready to terminate at the same time. At one such occasion, I felt as the captain of the Lusitania did when she went down: not that I had left the group, but that the group left me.

A definite sense of termination, like the sense of closure tells me when to agree with a patient who is reaching the terminal phase of treatment. If the patient has learned how to communicate freely and how to communicate with himself and others, or when he has gone as far as can be expected, then he may continue on his own. At times I consider termination a therapeutic necessity, like taking a plant out of a flower pot and planting it in the garden. Termination should be a growth experience.

TERMINATION AS A GROWTH EXPERIENCE

Recently, I have tried to turn termination into a therapeutic experience. I do not mean just the therapeutic pressure of setting a termination date. I mean more than that. I try to judge whether the patient is ready to terminate and to live without group and therapist and still continue to grow. Can he weather his separation anxiety without regression? Will he remain in free, spontaneous, responsive communication with himself and with his neighbors, with his own and with their unconscious? This communication should be more or less free of anxiety. If the separation can be handled successfully with additional insight then it is time to consider it. As with almost everything else in therapy, timing is of the essence.

Occasionally termination is a therapeutic necessity and a challenge to final maturation.

Tom had had a long record of therapy. He had almost become addicted to it. He had been dissatisfied with his work as an artist, gone into analysis, and later become a personnel manager. After his analysis he continued in a group of couples with a previous therapist for several years. When this analyst left town, Tom came to me where he continued for over three years in the same group together with his wife.

Halfway through the third year he began to talk in terms of terminating his treatment but changed his mind quickly and decided in favor of a lifelong learning experience which he pictured as continuous analytic group therapy to safeguard his further growth. This was a new idea for me and I was startled by it.

At the end of the third year he had his first peaceful and happy, almost triumphant, visit with his parents. They had now made peace with many of his decisions and with his firm intention to lead his own life. This peace was accomplished with understanding and without compromise. It had given him a feeling of peaceful triumph. There was a short period of sadness which ended in his joyful acceptance of his freedom. He then decided that now would be the time to discontinue his treatment. He had never had a chance to separate himself from his therapist. It had been the therapist who had left him.

The group had the usual negative reaction. Martin had lost his beloved enemy. Gustave tried hard but in vain to prove that the wish to leave was a sign of resistance and ought to be analyzed. Christopher would like to continue without Tom but have his wife present. The ladies started to arrange farewell parties. Rose got sick and had to lie down because she felt so hurt about Tom's desertion.

I agreed at first, silently thinking not only that it was time for Tom to terminate, but also that it was necessary. He had to feel that he could stand independently without parents, his own family, and the group. When he tried to postpone the termination date indefinitely, I set it for a date six weeks hence. He was shocked and angered, and then he agreed. Years later it seemed to have been the right timing.

A LAST DREAM

Gisela had decided to terminate after four years of faithful attendance. She had become a group therapy veteran and was the only member present at the start of this specific group. She hesitated to set a date for termination and broke into tears whenever she thought of it. She reported what she later called her "last dream": she was visiting a friend who had a baby already a year old. The mother never took it out of the crib and the dreamer was determined to take it out and let it crawl around since the crib was getting too small and restrictive.

The meaning of the dream was so obvious to everybody that it seemed unlikely the dreamer did not understand it. Nobody in the group was not ready with an interpretation, but the dreamer declared she had no idea what it was all about. The group offered the obvious interpretation, that it was about time to leave the crib, or the group, and go on her way by herself. That was then what she did.

THE THREAT OF TERMINATION

Once in a while, somebody brings himself in conflict with the entire group. Such a clash has to be analyzed, not bridged over or smoothed out; this has to be done immediately, before the group divides itself into subgroups.

Otto had begun to control his heavy drinking by the heavy use of marijuana. In order to support his expensive habit, he started to sell some to his friends and retained what he needed for himself. Finally he had established a flourishing trade, distributing marijuana. When the group learned about it, he was first warned and finally told that he would have to stop or would have to stop coming to the group. The group was not trying to protect him against the use of pot, which almost everybody in the group used occasionally. The group was concerned with the young man ruining his university career by being caught.

The peer pressure was strong enough to stop Otto from further trading and from returning to alcoholism.

TERMINATION BY DROPPING OUT

Some years ago during a group session, one woman said suddenly, "I could not go to sleep last week after our group, and instead of counting sheep I thought of all the people who have started here after

me and have left during the two-and-a-half years in which I have been
with this group. You know how many I remembered? Eighteen! I feel
like a veteran survivor."

I was shocked by the number eighteen in a group with an average
strength of six to eight participants. This group was started five years
ago and has been working continuously ever since. Searching through
my notes, which I take after every group session, I found to my surprise
that the woman had been correct in her count, although two of the
eighteen had been transferred to other groups and could be accounted
for as continuing therapy. I decided to investigate the statistics for all
my groups during the five years from April 1966 until the fall of 1971.

In these five years, I had started eight new groups. Of these eight
groups, I had terminated two, one of them being a training group and
the other a hospital group. This last group is not included in this report
because admittance, attendance, and termination of participation was
not determined by the individual but by the hospital administration.

Altogether 122 patients entered my groups. Of the original 122
members, 45 are still continuing treatment in six groups, and 34
terminated treatment after having attended group meetings regularly
for at least one and a half years, and usually for more than two years.
This leaves 43 patients who terminated group treatment after having
participated for less than one year. These are the people whom I shall
call "dropouts."

Of the 43 patients who discontinued their treatment, 24 were
male and 19 female. This approximately matches the composition of
my groups in which men tend to outnumber women. In studying
these dropouts, it appeared that they could logically be divided into five
categories.

Insufficient Motivation. The most numerous category of people
(thirteen) who discontinued treatment early can best be classified as
insufficiently motivated to continue the stress to be expected from
further group experience. Among the eight males in this category were,
to my surprise, five physicians. This is a high percentage but can be
explained by the fact that my groups contain quite a number of
physicians. I was surprised because of my unjustified assumption that
physicians ought to know better and should not have started if they
were not determined to follow through. Two of the physicians had
come for training purposes only and felt disappointed when they

realized that I considered therapy an essential part of training. Naturally, I had explained this in the beginning and they had accepted it readily, but when the analytic process threatened to deepen, they fled.

The majority of people included under insufficient motivation were patients for whom group therapy was a kind of crisis intervention treatment. It helped them to resolve their presenting symptoms, and after the emergency was relieved and before they could become members of an analytic group, they left.

Three of the thirteen people counted in this category were referred to me for consultation with a wish to start psychoanalysis. They came for a trial period to group therapy, and then when they preferred standard analysis they left the group and were referred into analysis.

Since most of these dropouts left newly formed groups, it is possible that I may have introduced new members without preparing them as carefully in individual treatment as I usually do. I am less anxious now to build up a newly formed group to full strength. Established, continuous groups have fewer dropouts than newly started groups.

Contraindications to Further Group Treatment.   Eleven patients discontinued treatment because of manifest or threatening psychotic breakdowns. Two had to be referred elsewhere because of unmanageable alcoholism. Four of the six men suffered from psychotic depression, were suicidal, and in need of hospitalization.

I had been aware of the diagnosis of all these patients when I invited them to join a group. I did not hide my concern and my doubt whether group therapy would be possible or whether it would have to be discontinued after a trial period. In each instance we started with good intentions but also with the knowledge that analytic group therapy would be more or less an experiment. All of these patients, paradoxically enough, did fairly well, especially the depressive ones, but the price for their improvement was paid by the group. When this became apparent, I grew reluctant to continue. In such situations, when one member of the group slips into a psychotic episode, the group tends to turn into a good, protective, understanding, collective mother. For a while this may be a maturing experience for everybody, but it soon inhibits the unfolding of unlimited free associative communication. At this point, I referred these patients into a hospital group. I did not conclude that these patients were generally unfit for group therapy, only that they belonged in differently structured groups than the ones conducted by me in my office.

Fear of Further Confrontation.   All seven people (four men and three women) of this category, came to the group because of conflicts in their marriages. During their treatment they increasingly realized that divorce was unavoidable, and they could not or would not face this possibility. These were usually people who had been married for a long time, about twenty years. They could neither face nor even discuss separation as an alternative to their misery. I would have expected this to be more often the fear of women than of men, but in this small number of people it was equally distributed between men and women.

In this category I counted two couples who did not feel that they could continue without hurting each other deeply. The suggestion that they continue treatment separately in two different groups was not acceptable.

External Circumstances.   In the part of the country in which I work, Southern California, a considerable number of people have had to leave to find work in other parts of the state. Members of a group are always ready to call such a reason a "resistance," but the reality of life comes first and treatment second.

Intensive Negative Transference and Reaction and Corresponding Negative Countertransference Reaction.   When I thought of patients who had left groups prematurely because of unmanageable or unanalyzable hostility, I could remember only two women. After carefully going through the records of all my patients who had ever been in any of my groups and dropped out, I realized that I had five patients during this period whose negative transference toward me was met with an undisguised negative countertransference reaction on my side, leading to termination.

Of the two men in this category, one was a colleague much younger than I, perhaps only half my age. I would classify him as an acting-out character who acted out not only in deeds but also in words. By this I mean that he did not follow the principle rule of group therapy which is to express himself not only frankly but also honestly to the best of his knowledge. He used words not to gain insight and be free, but to hurt, wound, depreciate, or to win an argument. Thus his outbursts were like acting out in the truest sense of the Freudian definition. By speaking so destructively he repeated his oedipal situation but did not learn from it. I hoped in vain that he would join me in a battle against that part of himself which caused sickness and suffering and pain. He was one of those people who fight their depression by giving it to others. I did not see any way to influence him other than to respond to him in kind in order to show him what he was doing. Such confrontation seemed unavoidable to me. The group became involved and locked in verbal battle. Every time a new provocation was unpacked, I had to choose between reacting to it or interpreting it. I tried both: I responded with interpretations, but when the man's provocation threatened the life of the group, I could not allow the session to become a battlefield for our reenactment of the Oedipus tragedy with the members of the group as onlookers.

The other male patient who succeeded in getting a strong negative reaction from me was equally young. He had spent several years in a concentration camp. When he told his story, he won the heart and the sympathy of everybody, and the tears of some. We all extended ourselves with compassion and offered loudly or silently our help in lessening the horrible suffering which had been the man's fate. During the months of treatment he developed a concentration camp transference in which he again was the victim, and I was supposed to play the role of the camp commander. This was such an intolerable transference assignment for me, being a refugee myself, that I did not feel that I could accept it. As in the case of the previous young man, I interpreted his behavior patiently and repeatedly. He intensified his transference and deepened his accusations, appealing to the sympathy of everybody, and then chose not to appear again after a vacation.

Two of the three women toward whom I developed an intense hostile reaction believed, and behaved accordingly, as if they knew everything better than anyone else, particularly the therapist. In order to confront them with their provocative, exhibitionist, masochistic conceit I got so involved in hostile responses that the work of the entire group was endangered. I always assumed that these women would at least recognize my good will, and I did not see any other way of dealing with them since it seemed to me that their treatment had to start with confrontation before they could gain any insight. Their behavior had become conflict-free to them, and I felt that it was my duty as a therapist to activate a conflict first. I certainly succeeded in doing that, but the conflict remained between them and me. It was fought out in the reality setting of the group instead of being introjected and felt as inner conflict. I assumed in vain that the decent, hidden part in them would join me in my offer of a therapeutic alliance against a common enemy.

The third woman in this category used the group meetings to express her flaming racial and political hatred, which got so disruptive that I had to ask her either to silently witness the group process until she understood it better or to resign, which she did.

With one exception, all members of this category came to me after years of analytic treatment by certified and established analysts. I therefore think that individual interviews, which I suggest now when premature termination of treatment threatens, would not have succeeded. The fact of previous treatment may have influenced my intolerance and impatience. I felt that these four people ought to have acquired more understanding for themselves, for me and for the therapeutic process during their previous treatment than to behave the way they did.

I found it necessary to show these patients that they did not know what a therapeutic confrontation really feels like. It was my impression that they had avoided such confrontation during their prolonged analytic treatment because they had placed their unknown and invisible analyst on a pedestal behind the couch, idealized and adored him, and never faced him in combat. I tried to involve them, with disastrous results as far as further treatment was concerned. I believe I have learned to be more patient and proceed more slowly in such situations but there are limits to my patience and these limits are set by the group process. When that is endangered the life of the group is endangered and my interference is required.

ARE THERE TRULY IMPOSSIBLE PEOPLE?

It took me a long time before I realized that there are people who are truly impossible in my groups and who could neither be treated by me nor tolerated by the group. I may have wasted some of my energy and some of the group's time before I recognized this type. I had to learn not to accept them into any group, not because they would be a challenge leading to defeat, but because they were genuinely unsuited for groups, just as some people are genuinely unfit for psychoanalysis. I cannot say whether these personality types constitute a true counter-indication to group therapy. Even for them the group experience would be of greatest value, if they only could find a group strong and patient enough to handle them.

The truly impossible person is compelled to interfere with the group process by different means. Most of these people are domineering, controlling, or manipulating. Occasionally this behavior can be analyzed and a confrontation with the group's reaction can be useful. Soon the therapist and his group come to the point where they have to decide whether to surrender their autonomy or to survive as a group. Since it is truly a fight for survival on both sides, the individual has to leave and let the group continue. During the terminal fight, these people enjoy a kind of triumph.

I have learned to recognize this personality type since they truly threaten the group cohesion of which I am the protector. I see in them the prototype of the bad mother who is endangering my group family and whom I have to fight.

In one of my groups a patient succeeded in antagonizing the entire group. He thought he was honest, frank, and revealing about his innermost secrets. He revealed things he had not even told his analyst in his previous analysis. The group responded with disgust and everybody made his response quite clear, with the result that the man declared, "What happened now is exactly what I expected to happen. When I really and truthfully reveal myself, I am rejected. I will stop being honest." Triumphantly, he added "I shall quit the group."

My interpretation was clear, outspoken, and forcefully offered. "Your behavior is not honest, frank and spontaneous. Your behavior is a masochistic provocation and an exhibitionistic performance. You behave like a baby who quietly assumes his mother will love him even if he has dirtied his diapers. We do not think you are a baby, do not expect nor want your dirtiness. We understand your behavior is your provocative plea for acceptance at all costs by us. We gladly accept you and we gladly try to understand you, but not on these terms 'You must love me anyhow.'" The patient preferred his masochistic indulgence to analytic insight and when the clash grew louder and the rift deeper, he dropped out, convinced that he had won his point. Actually only a self-fulfilling prophecy had come true.

WHICH DROPOUTS WERE PREDICTABLE, AND WHICH ONES WERE AVOIDABLE?

Eighteen of the forty-three dropouts were predictable, seven may have been avoidable in retrospect, and eighteen came as a disappointing surprise.

Many of the dropouts could have been predicted and had actually been predicted. This is also true for their instances of successful crisis intervention and for those people with psychotic episodes. In all these cases I had great doubts whether the patients would outlast the three month trial period of treatment. I felt that they should be given the chance, and I still feel the same way. I will be only slightly more selective in the future.

Different from the predictable dropouts were the ones which could have been avoided if I had known then what I know now. These were people whom I should have invited to more intensive preparatory individual treatment. I have developed this technique now to a definite method for which the indication is simply the need of the patient for more therapeutic time than the group can give him. It should be noted, however, that with a few of these dropouts termination could probably not have been avoided because they would have refused an invitation for personal interviews too.

A prolonged individual period of preparation is especially indicated for isolated, sensitive, schizoid persons who need to develop a close relationship to the central figure before they can be expected to form a workable relation to the group.

COMPARING DROPOUTS WITH PATIENTS WHO TERMINATE AFTER LONG PARTICIPATION

It seems that my best patients in group are middle-aged male psychotherapists. They seek treatment because they are mildly depressed, feel isolated, and have developed serious doubts about their therapeutic efficacy.

They work on their problems patiently and consider the group process as that kind of learning experience which should not necessarily be terminated. They stay, as a rule for a period of three years, before they are ready for either a definite termination or a prolonged interruption. The door is always left open for their return if the need arises.

My most difficult patients are middle-aged, female psychotherapists who seem to know everything better. They claim to be full of respect and recognition but consider it their divine duty to put me in my place. An observer might suggest patience, endurance, stubborn repetition of interpretation, consistent confrontation, and all the tools of analytic therapy. But their drive to dominate is stronger than the tools of our gentle art, stronger than the combined effort of me and the group. They depart in triumphant defeat.

The most annoying patients are young psychiatrists who seem to come exclusively in order to look almost with pity at my – to them – obvious inability to conduct group therapy. When I speak, I should have been silent; when I am silent, I should have spoken. Out of a hundred possible interpretations, I chose the only wrong one. When I dramatize a conflict, I should have played it down; and when I am cool, I should have responded with deeply felt emotion. When I go on a vacation, I should have stayed; and when I return, I should have stayed away. Still, they continue to come, to learn, and at times even to grow. Some of them do drop out but their number is relatively small. I have checked my clinical impression of an especially intense hostility of younger psychiatrists with other group therapists and find that it is universally true. A young professional group is similar to Freud's Ur-Horde; it is out to kill the father, devour him, and then finally to love him.

THE KICK-OUT

Premature termination is not an event that happens exclusively between patient and therapist or within the patient. It includes the dynamics of the entire group.

It has happened that a group does not accept a new member but consistently rejects him. If this is the case, it can fairly well be assumed that the new patient is truly impossible and that he must face this in painful confrontation. Group rejection is rare because there is hardly a human being who is unacceptable to all members of the group. As a rule, the group is a truly good and strong mother, in fantasy and in reality.

A variation of the dropout is the kick-out. In two cases the patient did not want to leave the group but was told in definite terms to get out.

In the first case, a man played a self-assigned role representing the bad mother (or the bad parent) so well that the group reacted in loud rebellion and invited the bad father-mother to leave.

The second situation was quite different. The new member did not offer herself as a bad mother but as the baby. She maneuvered the group to behave like a rejecting mother.

THE OPEN-ENDED NATURE OF ALL THERAPY

All therapy should be open ended. The doors should be left open so that every patient can feel free to return. This is not a sign of failure for the patient, for his group, or for the therapist.

9

Some Additional
Clinical Observations

The aim of the group experience is to help the individual to become a conscious, direct, frank, honestly communicating person who begins to understand himself, his unconscious and that of others and who responds to others spontaneously and without anxiety and fear about his need for intimacy or aggression.

The group experience should help a person live in harmony with himself, with others, and with nature. The process of individuation consists of a realization of the person's potential.

The goal is to live the free life motivated by the desire to know, think, and act as conscience demands – to move out of neurosis into being one's self without hurting others.

THE STRUCTURE OF ANALYTIC GROUPS

A group which works together for several years assumes a certain characteristic structure which is different from that of other groups. Even when the original pioneer-patients with whom I started a group are long gone and have been replaced with newcomers, this character remains largely unchanged.

My week's first group meeting used to take place on Tuesday morning with a group of senior psychiatrists who wished to work together in one group without outsiders. They wanted to discuss without embarrassment or defensiveness, their doubt and sometimes their cynicism about their profession. They all complained about their isolation, their frustration in their work, and in their families.

The evening of the same day used to belong to a group of young people and was nicknamed "the kindergarten." The average age of the group members was younger than that of other groups.

People who were the masters of their time were collected on Wednesday at noon in a group which was kiddingly called "Hollywood Nobility." Their successful careers made it possible for them to interrupt their working day for the group sessions.

A special character developed in a group which came from out of town after the sudden death of their therapist in order to continue their work together. The character of this group was definitely different from any other group. The assignment of mourning was only the start of our work and the group continued for several years with little changes in membership.

The Thursday evening group was my smallest group consisting of three men and three women. They all happened to be utterly unrelated people, alienated even from themselves, seemingly indifferent, but actually extremely sensitive. Their schizoid character was the main reason for their consulting me. This group began finally to develop a certain group cohesion when I became less active, less desperate, and more relaxed, waiting for things to happen instead of trying to stimulate interaction. I am no longer worried that every member may remain for himself and that they may never form a group.

Later when I made a special effort to find the reasons for the slowness of this group, I realized that it was my selection of patients which kept this group seemingly stalemated. Each time I was consulted by another unrelated person, I unfailing invited him into this group. I did not distribute these people carefully into different groups where they could be carried along for a while without slowing down the group process until they could start relating better.

A second afternoon group was an equally worrisome problem

group and was called by me in my silent inner language with that label for a long time. It was a group of three indecisive men and three sad, depressed, often silent women. At the first opportunity, I introduced two active and loudly complaining men. One of them suffered from a compulsive obsessive neurosis and the other was an intensive, acting-out, impulsive character. Their almost miraculous progress in the group changed the sterile therapeutic atmosphere and I had one less group to worry about.

The hospital group on Friday morning consisted of twenty-five hospitalized patients – most of them psychotic – and the entire professional and nursing staff of the ward. Obviously such a group looks and interacts differently from other groups.

I add new members to that group in which I expect them to work best. For a while I assumed that a member who does not fit into a group becomes a problem to be solved by the group. I thought that this should not be avoided or corrected by selection. Recently however, I have changed my opinion and invite new members to join a group where I think they will help form a specific cohesive and well-working family.

I always try to keep the sexes equally distributed but I often have a surplus of men. Once I had to work for a while with a group of six men and one woman. She was never happier in all her life, and the men enjoyed the situation too.

SPONTANEOUS RESPONSIVE INTERACTION AS THE ESSENCE OF THE THERAPEUTIC GROUP PROCESS

Some years ago (1968), Natterson and I published a paper on responsive interaction in psychotherapy. It was – and still is – our opinion that in many and perhaps all therapeutic situations, interpretations must be fortified by specific responsive action by the therapist. It is probable that most therapists carry out such responsive action, but they may be unaware that they are doing so, or they may feel guilty about it, when in fact they are exerting a powerfully effective and legitimate therapeutic interaction.

Responsive interaction is a term which characterizes the therapist's reaction to the patient's unconscious needs, as distinguished from his conscious wishes or desires. The therapist's responsive interaction should be genuine and spontaneous. At all times the responsive inter-action should derive from the therapist's basic reaction to the patient's basic need. The responsive interaction may consist only of an emo-tional coloring which the therapist subtly injects into the session, or it may consist of an unmistakable emotional response.

Effective responsive action should be based upon accurate and constant appraisal of the transference–countertransference situation and the unconscious need indicated by it. Responsive interaction makes a therapeutic situation human. The therapeutic efficiency of family treatment is based to a large extent upon the therapist's greater freedom to respond more spontaneously and actively in a triangular situation than he would allow himself to in a one-to-one relationship.

Advice is a concrete example of responsive action. Other forms include the use of humor, sympathy, affection, closeness, disapproval, or even restrained hostility; the form, content, and timing of questions and the formality or informality of a particular situation may be influenced. Thus, the responsive action may be concrete and obvious or it may be subtle.

Responsive interaction varies according to the character and personality of therapist and patient. It also changes with the thera-peutic situation and with the phase of treatment.

A therapist may attempt to avoid a realistic relationship toward the patient, preferring to remain a transference figure only. If the patient does not permit this, responsive action inevitably emerges. This was well expressed by Greenson, when he once asked, "Who wants to be analyzed by a blank screen anyhow?"

Responsive interaction in groups is not, as in psychoanalysis, limited to two people, and it is not limited to the therapist's response to the group of patients. In the group, everybody is responding con-stantly, spontaneously, and honestly. It presupposes a genuine and general human gift for interaction. In the group, a therapist is mostly concerned with watching and at times interpreting the responses of almost everybody to almost everybody else.

Spontaneity and responsiveness are the expression of the group's common bond and its common language. Continued responsiveness grows out of the matrix, the network of communication of which it is a function.

The group develops a definite feeling for the needs of its members and, if well conducted, develops this sensitivity to an ever higher degree in the course of group work.

Responsive action can be hidden in many different disguises. It may be emotional or it may lead to advice and counsel, which is often a different form of interpretation. I feel the needs of my patients and respond to them. I do not respond to conscious wishes which have to remain unfulfilled in a transference situation.

I have learned to have trust and confidence in the basic nature and function of the matrix in the group. This leads to analysis of the group by the group. It has nothing to do with common sense which is a combination of many defenses.

The ability to be spontaneous and interpretative in responsive interaction is dependent on my belief in the basic goodness of people. The intent to help is a capability of life, of humans, of everybody, activated in the therapeutic group and deepened by the understanding which we call analytic.

Most of the members of this group arrived fifteen minutes before the hour and waited in the waiting room. It is the only one of my groups which has the habit of arriving that early. I opened the door to the consultation room as always, ten minutes before the hour.

Christopher singled me out and showed me a letter from a friend we have in common in London. She had sent him two of her manuscripts about Shakespeare. In a note she described herself as an "Honorary Member of the Group."

Sophia, the newest member of the group, already well liked and accepted, had had a bad week. She was deeply hurt that Sylvia had said to her, "You compete with Karla for the affection of Grotjahn." Sophia had been the oldest of seven brothers and sisters and had learned early in her life to share. She always had worked hard, became the right hand to her mother at home and to her father in his business. She did not feel that she had ever abused her privileged position as Sylvia implied – an accusation she had heard so often in her life. Obviously Sylvia's remark had activated an old guilt. Sophia had always felt hated by her mother for her favored place in her father's affection. This was actually the reason why, in later life, Sophia left work in her father's factory and made herself independent in her own career. She handed her father back to her mother and wanted to do that now with the therapist, handing him back to Sylvia.

Sylvia in turn responded that she was envious and jealous and intended to cut Sophia down. Before Sophia had arrived in the group, Karla seemed to have enjoyed the undivided favor of the therapist and she, Sylvia, wanted to protect her friend. Recently Sylvia had felt utterly neglected by the therapist. After several years of a sterile marriage, she had finally become pregnant. She had written her father about it, and he did not even bother to answer. Nobody ever approved of her.

I reluctantly agreed that I kept a careful distance from her. "As you know, I was against your pregnancy. Your husband has four children from his previous marriage, the youngest one of them ready for college. I did not even believe you were pregnant.

"Now I have to reorient myself as your husband will have to reorient himself. He is ahead of me, and I shall follow suit. There is no doubt that both of us will come around, but it will take a little time. Soon we will join in your happiness."

Christopher interrupted here to tell a dream. "A woman was sitting on the side of the road on which I was walking and laughed at me. I woke up and felt the laughter in my throat." As it is his habit, he did not want to give any associations or any clues. He just gave us the dream, sat there and expected us to come up with some startling interpretation. When we all waited for him invitingly, he said that he is afraid we all disapproved of his plans for marriage, in which he expected great happiness and final fulfillment. His wife-to-be was twenty years younger and perhaps an old man should not marry so young a woman. Everybody would laugh.

I responded by saying: "The laughing lady at the roadside was our friend in London whom you met and who once discussed the psychology of laughter with me. I told you the story of how she was fighting in the underground and saw the German troops running to escape and how that made her laugh so hard that she dropped her gun. My friend in the dream also represented me, whom you fear will disapprove of your plans and will laugh at you. It implies that you want to see me run like the defeated Germans." Now Christopher felt free to talk about his own doubts about his marriage. The group's final response: It is possible that you have slowly become ready in your life to accept intimacy, warmth, love and even happiness. A number of years have gone by, and our hopes for you have come true to an astonishing degree.

Tom continued where Christopher left off: "I too had a dream which was repeated several times with slight variation. Gustave told me to buy a new house and to furnish it any way I wanted. Money should make no difference. I bought an old-fashioned long sofa with a love seat on one end, writing desk in the middle, and something else on the far end." The group responded to Tom's dream by saying approximately: "You hope and you realize that we all will recognize your right to a new house, a new wife, and a new affluency. We, your elders, should pledge not to take it from you."

Tom had taken much time in previous hours talking about his anxiety, his ever deepening relationship to his new wife, and his new business. He did not feel neglected, but Sylvia did. During this time Karla had said nothing. She was sitting there as if quietly enjoying the show.

At this point I turned to Martin who in the previous session had been outraged at me and threatened to kill me. "Hey, come on, don't wait until the last minute and then explode and we are all shocked and surprised!" Martin followed the invitation and told the story of the weekend. He had gone hunting but he couldn't shoot a deer and face her eyes. So he decided to shoot only pheasants. "I was shooting nothing. Every time a bird flew up in front of me I was doing something else and missed my chance. Finally we drove home and drank beer. When I got home I was drunk. My wife was not especially sympathetic the next morning when I felt like dying." His story was funny and sad – but also significant for so angry a man who feared that he could grow violent or run berserk.

The group wished that we could help Martin more. We always went with him to the edge of his rage and then did not know how to proceed. I said that I would like to go on an African safari with him and shoot an elephant, and then we would take the elephant apart looking for his heart. I followed through with gruesome details of this bloody fantasy. Tom joined Martin's rage and my fantasy by saying to me, "You want him to act out? Do you think it would help him to do something? Perhaps murder you?"

I said, "No, I am trying to dream for him and to have a nightmare. I want to dramatize his bloody fantasies for him. I want to show him that I know what goes on in him and in you too, Tom. You two don't need to be afraid, here we can handle your rage. There is nothing to fear. He can handle his unconscious and so can you; at least we can face it and you will feel better about yourself. You may even feel purified. From there it will take only one more step to get to the decisive point— how easy it is for Martin to get in contact with his hostility and rage and how difficult and frightening it is for him to allow himself to feel his tenderness and love. These he can feel only, so to speak, 'after he shot the deer.' "

While Martin allowed the interpretation to sink in, Tom followed our line of association and began to talk about his father. He did the work Martin was not yet willing to do.

Finally near the end of the hour, Karla came to life and joined the group process for the first time in this session. She reported about her visit to friends. Their teenage son was so obnoxious, naughty, and destructive that she finally hit him with a pillow, to everybody's surprise. Then the father was indignant about it so she hit the boy again with the pillow. The group immediately got the message and related this incident to her husband Tom and his friend Martin. Boys have to be aggressive and then mother helps them to control it. Then they can allow a little loving to be expressed.

It is difficult to demonstrate the free-floating, spontaneous, and responsive communication which takes place in such an hour. Any summary or abstract distorts the gestalt of the happening.

The hour was an illustration of an old truth: nobody is as bad as he fears to be and nobody is as good as he hopes to be.

Big Bill started by telling how his wife returned with the children from a visit to her parents. He had been alone for two weeks and greeted her full of love and tenderness and promised to make a sincere effort to come closer to her. He thought this would be a final break-through, and he told her so while driving home from the airport. She remained silent and cold and unmoved and said finally: "Too late."

He felt a wild fury and told her so. When he turned to her, he found her deep asleep. He decided to live together with her in the same house but to go on his own way from then on.

Each one of the group responded with sympathy, each one in his own way. Myron considered his marriage situation to be like Bill's. Benvenuto realized that he had divorced his wife after thirty years of marriage because a well-mannered distance had developed between her and him, and it was no longer satisfying. He had formed a new relationship and this seemed to progress in the same way, and he would have to dissolve it too. He had to free himself for a truly felt love he never had experienced.

Marion, who had difficulties in joining the group, tried to confirm her insecure understanding by endless questions, until brusquely stopped by someone who resented this kind of ungiving intrusion.

Rita, who had been caught in an ugly divorce situation, said quietly to Bill: "Don't decide anything because of her. Do what you really feel like doing regardless of her. If you love her don't stop it now because she seemed difficult. When my husband wanted to come back, I told him also 'Too late.' I hope you stand the test as my husband did not. You must really do whatever you feel in your heart like doing, regardless of her testing you."

It was moving to all of us to hear how this young woman, left by her husband with two small children, now involved in a vicious divorce suit, found these words of enduring love, of a woman who recognized a mistake she had made. Emotions like these must be witnessed in the group session to feel their impact on everybody.

I had responded to Bill by discussing whether it was now time for him and his wife to sleep in separate bedrooms. I did not consider this a first step to final separation but perhaps the first step to gaining a new perspective on each other. Myron reacted with doubts to my remark. Similar advice given to him by me ten years ago was the straw which broke his previous marriage. I remembered the story of his divorce quite differently and wanted to hear more about his opinion, but the group considered this unimportant and beside the point of the day, and we moved on.

Judy made a visible effort to join the group and to overcome a feeling of being inferior to everybody. She always had to force herself to speak, and then she went into all the details, which was annoying to everybody. I responded to her and said, "Your inferiority feelings developed out of your dissatisfaction with your marriage and your life. You were a good wife to your husband, a good mother to your children, a good daughter to your father, and now you try to be a good patient here. You never liberated your husband from his isolation. You left him mostly alone as he left you alone. You feel inferior because you have not taught your husband the one great lesson a woman has to give, to allow himself to feel his love to you. Stop giving all those details. You want to give us an objective report, an eye witness account, so that we can judge you fairly as a jury in a trial is supposed to do. This is not our assignment. What you say is not a question of right or wrong, but a question of understanding. Stop being good. Start being yourself."

Without giving Judy a chance to respond to that Carol apologized for having to break in; she had to tell about a great catastrophe of the last week. She went with her husband to a party which obviously was the beginning of a promising swinging party. She always had thought of herself as being tough, but she was now more and more impressed by her vulnerability: "I always have been called upon for help. I was the strong one. In my first marriage and in my second." When she saw that her husband reacted to the seduction of the swingers, she was beside herself with rage and fear and ran out and smashed the window of his car with her hand. She went home and got sick with the flu. It was not clear to her whether she was so furious at herself, at her husband, or at the temptation she herself felt, followed by frustration.

The group took this story without much of a reaction. We did not feel like judging, warning, or supporting her. The consensus of opinion was when you play with fire you probably will get burned.

THE DEPTH OF THE THERAPEUTIC PROCESS

Martin opened the session by talking about a terrible attack of claustrophobia. He had to fly in the company plane with five people who work with him. The airplane could carry only six people. He had flown in the same plane several times, and had always taken a tranquilizer before and had no anxiety. Then he decided it would be time to try it without the pill. At first everything went well on the forty-five minute flight but then he was overcome with a twofold anxiety. He felt he would glide from his seat and fall off the plane and had to lean away from the window, almost across his neighbor. Then he feared he would run wild or faint or would holler and scream to bring the plane down. Nothing happened but he arrived a nervous wreck, drenched in sweat.

Martin had catapulted himself recently to the peak of his career and never felt better about his work. He had only recently started this new job, being well liked by everybody, slowly taking on the responsibility of a boss. He had much less anxiety and was no longer really bothered by the fear of driving off the highway. However, he had not tested his strength, and occasionally thought how easy it would be to provoke his old fears.

The group had already given him an interpretation of his inner rage. The fear of running off the freeway disguised the wish to use his car as a deadly missile and fly it like a suicide bomber into the roof of the next house and kill the father sitting there. The fantasy provided a built-in punishment, since he would probably not live through such a spectacularly destructive display.

The group responded to the claustrophobic attack in the plane with a similar interpretive response. We all were familiar with the inner rage of this elegant and well-mannered, young business executive who was the perfect son any boss could wish to have around. Once in a while he had to explode.

Another member reported about an anxiety attack while sailing, which was relieved by seasickness. Somebody else remembered how he fainted once when a big boat was christened by a distinguished visitor. On the moment of the bottle crashing against the boat he fainted dead away without being noticed by anybody, to his relief and disappointment.

While listening to Martin's story, I remembered how when visiting New York once, I had met Eleanor Roosevelt, who took me to the top of the Empire State Building, overlooking the city. It was a high point in my life. I remembered so well how I had entered America only a few years before through the Port of New York and now I was standing with the widow of the President of the United States, on top of the world. I could enjoy this triumph without guilt, without fear of punishment, while Martin with his unsettled conflict and ambivalence to his father considered any success as a murderous assault deserving immediate punishment.

Martin responded to this interpretation with some more associations and recollections of his childhood and his lifelong struggle with his father who had taken the place of the mother in Martin's affection. The real mother remained in the background. For him and everybody in the group it was important to realize that the rage against the father also included rage against the mother, who did not love him enough to protect him. He had to stand up against the father all by himself.

Much of the time was taken up by listening to Martin and responding to him. Everybody participated in his anxiety, felt his own, applied Martin's insight to his own unconscious, as Martin deepened his own insight by listening to the others, including me. Christopher, for instance, had said little, but at the end of the hour he revealed that he never felt more intensively about his father and his therapist as in this hour – and never understood it better.

A peculiar change could be observed in Martin during the second half of the session. After we had already turned away from him, he displayed an unusual and remarkable and for me surprising insightful behavior. It was as if he had experienced a breakthrough into his unconscious and suddenly saw clearly the unconscious of other members of the group. He could not only give interpretations but could also illustrate them with quotations of the group interaction in previous hours. He talked as if he had taken tape recordings of those hours and replayed them now. For many months to come, Martin continued to show this remarkable and sensitive understanding. Occasionally he even analyzed my interaction with the group with startling insight and correctness.

Later, during the same session, Karla talked about a week of nightmares. She had been dreaming about blood and feces, it was terrible. She associated her nightmares with her attitude toward me. She always felt greatly tempted by father figures and here for the first time in her life a father figure said no to her attempts at seduction. She felt great relief and terrible frustration which did not let her sleep. She always felt that her intense feeling for her father was simultaneously stimulated and forbidden by her mother.

Karla's story was not directly interpreted by anyone in the group. The theme of erotized transference was however taken over by every woman and continued into the next meeting.

A TRULY MISERABLE HOUR

It started with my not feeling well. Possibly I had the flu. However, I had had an excellent group meeting in the morning, as it sometimes happens when I feel slightly sick. Now we just did not get off the ground. It had occurred to me on previous occasions that this group could be called my problem group. On this day I started to worry in earnest and tried to find the reasons for the slow and hesitant interaction. I concluded that the problem must be the composition of this group.

I thought I had a good working alliance with everybody. However, nobody allowed this relationship with me to include the group and everybody remained desperately isolated. Even the girls were truly unrelated in life and in the group. Their pseudohostility took the place of a real relationship.

Ed was preoccupied with his grief about his sick son, and Dora was quitting her job, leaving her house and group, and going on a world cruise of indefinite duration until she had spent her small savings.

I had hoped to bring life into these unrelating people at first with the help of Andrew who played the madman and frightened everybody including himself. In a couple of weeks he had quieted down and nothing much happened with him either.

Then I added Marlene because of her loud, hyperactive, and provocative behavior. I hoped she would bring at first motion, then emotion, to us, possibly later developing group interaction. She turned out to be a total loss to us. She assumed herself to be my helper and acted most stupidly and with such arrogant hostility that the whole group turned against her. It was just not possible to get interaction by attacking and criticizing only.

Provocative behavior is no help to the group and is only misleading since it leads to discipline before understanding. The result was defense and counterattack, no insight, no progress, and no real human relationship either. Marlene changed and tried the role of the group's Mother Superior by giving everybody advice, including telling us where to go for dinner since she considered herself to be a gourmet guide. She was a teacher, a governess, and at best a seducer – totally unfit to play the role of a mother to anybody.

Still acting under the assumption that I could activate this bunch of utterly unrelated people, I invited Antoinette as a catalyst. She promptly launched a private liaison with Marlene resulting in a conspiracy and secret communication between the two.

Liza was living in another world, commuting from there only with flippancies, to her own embarrassment. She felt unworthy and guilty that she was not a good wife to her husband; now she was developing a similar guilt toward us for not being a more responsive member of the group. Nevertheless she had changed since she came to the group. Recently she had again settled in emptiness.

Henry was so alienated from all reality that he was going to lose his wife. We predicted that he would mourn less about her than when his cat ran away for a day.

It so happened that I had seen Henry's and Andrew's wives in the morning hours of the same day in another group. That was of considerable help in my relationship to all four. However, when I made some remarks or asked some questions, they fell flat, and nothing was taken further. There was little interaction, little emotional cohesion, everybody was for himself, told his story and then after a moment of silence the next one did the same, unresponsive, unrelated to each other. The session usually started with Andrew telling his bizarre adventure of the week. Then I compared his story with his wife's report, carefully not betraying any confidence. This led logically to Henry and my connecting his story with that of his wife. Not knowing the wives, the group felt left out and a subgroup was formed between these two men, their wives and me.

Once more I tried to improve the character of the group discussion by introducing a new member who looked and behaved as if she would be the proverbial good nurse-mother to everybody. After the first meeting, on sudden impulse, she had invited the entire group to a Sunday afternoon in her apartment. After that Vivian turned resolutely from being the mother to symbolizing the baby of the group, crying loudly to be fed.

The most peculiar observation about the whole group was that everybody nevertheless felt much relieved from loneliness and nobody left the group. I was often the only one who was not satisfied. So I finally learned to stop complaining and to try waiting – advice which I probably would have given any beginner working with groups a long time ago.

During the weeks and months that followed, I was resigned, became less active, and more and more tolerant. In my silent, inner language I compared my behavior with that of Jane Goodall toward her chimpanzees. In the beginning of her research Jane Goodall was anxiously and actively running to come close to her chimpanzees. When she got sick and unable to run after them, they turned and came close to her.

This technique combined with further changes in the composition of the group finally succeeded and this group after a long and slow beginning is now proceeding as well as any other. I also realized at that time that I had, completely unknown to myself, used this group as a kind of dumping ground for people who had given me some doubts whether they could work in groups at all. This is a bad principle with which to select and compose groups and it did not happen again after I became aware of it.

LAUGHTER IN GROUPS

Although therapists do not cry with their patients and do not rage with them – or at them – we do feel free to laugh with them. Something is very wrong with a therapy group in which there is no laughter.

THE JOKE AS AN INTERPRETATION

Jokes can be an effective method of interpreting. The strength of American humor is the wisecrack, and the group is a fertile field for that. A wisecrack can be a pointed interpretation which pierces resistance with lightning speed.

One patient in a group complained consistently and bitterly about repeated, vicious fights between her and her husband. No matter how the group responded or what we said, suggested, interpreted, or advised, nothing helped, and the bitter fighting went on. Finally the group therapist said, "Do you know that on Noah's Ark sexual intercourse was forbidden? When the couples filed out of the Ark after the Flood, Noah watched them leave. Finally the tomcat and the she-cat left, followed by a number of very young kittens. Noah raised his eyebrows questioningly, and the tomcat said to him: 'You thought we were fighting?' " After that, the group cut short the woman's description of the marital fighting, implying that, if that was the way she wanted to live and love, then she should do so and not complain.

If a patient considers a joke inordinately funny, analysis of his exaggerated amusement may give a clue to what he does not dare to say directly. A patient was working well, and I summarized my impression of him near the end of the hour. The patient was duly impressed and went away seemingly appreciative. The next time he arrived shaking with laughter and immediately started to repeat a joke he had heard: "Three men were going on a fishing trip. It was agreed that one of them was to work as cook until somebody complained and then the complainer should take his turn. Naturally, there were no complaints. Finally, one morning one of the men could not stand it any more and turned to the cook and said: 'This really tastes like horseshit – but good!' " The patient could not have symbolized better the conflict between his appreciation for the insight gained and his intention to reject it as indigestible.

In individual therapy, the joke is between therapist and patient, while in the group situation the therapist may remain a witness and not be a party to it, which makes it easier for him to interpret the message in the joke. For example, at a time before I was against all smoking in my office, a man turned to a woman in the group who annoyed him by her heavy smoking and said, "You really ought to stop smoking." Thereupon, the woman answered: "Young man, I will be seventy next month, so what does it matter?" The dialogue was concluded with the young man having the last word: "If you had stopped smoking, you would be eighty by now."

Once a member of a group came twenty minutes late and another member turned to him and said caustically, "I hear you had a motor-boat accident while taking your morning walk," implying that the man seemed to view himself as capable of walking on water.

JOKING AS RESISTANCE

The telling of jokes and anecdotes is limited in its usefulness. Often the group will realize this and stop it, but if not, the therapist must intervene, which is relatively easily done by nonparticipation. A well working group has a built-in discipline, and almost everybody will oppose the clown and slowly wean him or her from the obsessive need to entertain instead of to reveal.

LAUGHTER AT THE UNMASKING OF
THE UNCONSCIOUS

There is one form of laughter in which I do not participate. This is laughter at the unmasking of the unconscious. This form of laughter occurs when people begin to understand the unconscious.

It was this kind of laughter in the Wednesday seminar evenings in Sigmund Freud's house which were studied by Freud and Theodor Reik, and which gave the first insight into the dynamics of laughter.

An example of this type of laughter occurred in a group when I wanted to say, "I cannot be a friend to everybody," but slipped by saying, "I cannot be a Freud to everybody." A roar of laughter greeted the slip. The group had caught me in a hidden confession of megalomanic ambition. A more harmless example was that of a woman patient who brought a newly planted shoot of an exotic plant to the group meeting. She looked at it with obvious delight and exclaimed in complete innocence, "It looks familiar, but what is it." The joyful laughter of the group made it clear that she had reacted to the phallic appearance of the plant while trying to deny it.

Group therapy is not a laughing matter, but neither is it a wailing wall.

HIGHLIGHTS OF GROUP WORK

I cannot resist recollecting a few remarks which impressed me when they sprang from the matrix of the group into the light of verbal communication. They are reported here as illustrations for the genuine and creative gifts of almost everybody for understanding his fellow men. In none of the following vignettes do I function as a speaker, but I am occasionally the target. I usually control my wit and my delight in the pointed formulation while working. A narcissistic, exhibitionistic therapist is not the best therapist. He endangers the group process by turning the group into an audience and the interaction into a performance.

In published reports about individual therapy, it often appears as if the patient delivers the associative material and the therapist interprets it. This is an exaggeration but it is certainly different from group therapy where the two functions are equally distributed among all. The flow of the discussion and its interpretation should be carried by all. I will try to illustrate this:

A small, sad, and usually silent woman regularly attended her group. She had recently lost her mother and four weeks later her husband, ending a marriage which had lasted over thirty years. She once listened to the story of another woman who contemplated leaving her husband, the father of her two children. The group had some doubts, but the widow said quietly, almost as if addressing herself: "Get yourself a divorce from your husband while he is still alive. When he is dead it is too late." These words contain the whole impact of the conflict between guilt, sadness, and shattered hope for a new beginning.

A man complained resignedly about his business. All that he wanted was some sympathy, but he got advice from his wife who knew everything better. The man listened nonplussed and said, "Wives who are not in the business are the enemies of the people."

A handsome Don Juan of a man looked with appreciation at an attractive girl and remarked to his neighbor, an all-time loser, "They all are waiting for us!" This firm belief gave him strength, courage and success.

A therapist in another group once gave a startling definition of creativity: The creative effort is an attempt to restore the destroyed mother with the help of an identification with the father.

Quite generally I would agree with the surprising comparative interpretation offered once in a group, "In Europe there are fathers and in America everybody has a mother."

A woman somewhat older than the average member of her group summarized her opinion about the younger people: Once a child always a child, or adults are the best children.

Many good and true things have been said about therapy, and therapists. Here are two:
A patient said looking back at his previous therapeutic experience, "Nobody should have only one therapist."
In another group with several therapist-members, one of them addressed a colleague by saying reassuringly, "In psychiatry you cannot be judged by your mistakes."

A WORD ABOUT THE FUTURE

Anyone who is not concerned about the future does not deserve to have one. Furthermore, our view of the future is no longer what it used to be. We are no longer driven by necessity only. We now need to clarify what we want and then to realize it. There is no time to lose since the future rushes upon us with ever increasing speed and we live in a time of rapid changes. What we need is a "future adjusted man."

I believe that therapy of the individual will mostly take place in groups. I believe that psychotherapy will not remain in the hands of physicians. A new specialty will develop and that is the specialty of the doctor of psychotherapy. There will be few physicians left in our field, partly in the function of what used to be called "neuropsychiatrists," specializing in "psycho-pharmacology." Other physicians will become team leaders, consultants, supervisors, and teachers. They may become therapists for therapists.

All psychotherapy will remain dynamic and in this sense will remain analytic (or motivation oriented). All therapy will operate with the basic concepts of the unconscious, resistance, interpretation, transference and insight, but the standard analysis as we know it today will become limited to training for members of the healing profession. Standard analysis will also remain a method of scientific investigation.

In the future therapists, not patients, will have to be analyzed. In this respect psychoanalysis will complete a circle. Analytic development started with the self-analysis of Sigmund Freud, moved to the psychoanalysis of patients, then to the training analysis for analysts. The treatment of patients will mostly take place in the form of analytic group therapy and its variations. These groups will be as different from each other as people are different. Groups will not be homogenous, but there will be groups for young and for old, for children and for adolescents; there will be analytic nurseries where the analyst goes from child to child, not taking them out of the group.

There will no longer be a question: group or not group? The question will always be, which group? There will be groups for homosexuals, for suicidal depressions, for couples and for unmarried people. There will be sessions with all kinds of different time arrangements: there will be the slow and steady working through in psychoanalytic group therapy which I consider the most effective form of therapy. Groups will meet in hospitals, in schools, in churches, in prisons, and in business offices, in factories, universities and in private offices. They will meet in villas in resort towns or on boats. Each time the transference situation will be different and will respond to the unconscious needs of the participants but not necessarily to their conscious wishes.

There will be active sex groups about which we would be as horrified today as the medical men of Vienna were when Sigmund Freud started to explain his newly gained insights into the unconscious. They will aim at something like a corrective primal scene experience.

There will be a place for individual interviews. The diagnostic interviews will develop into psychotherapy in order to establish that kind of working alliance between patient and therapist which must have been established before the patient is referred into the group. There will be individual time for crisis intervention when the patient needs more time than he can expect as his share in a group.

The coming age will be an age of learning and psychotherapy will be a part of it. People will insist on the right to be healthy in the sense of well-being. They will also demand the right to be unique and even peculiar. The group may replace the family – or at least supplement it – and therapy may become a way of life. Only the mind of the group and only collective intelligence will be able to cope with the problems of the future.

There will be abuse of group therapy. There will be spiritual supermarkets and there will be mental hygiene centers like filling stations all over the countryside. People without psychotherapy will be marked men as the insane used to be marked in the past.

These difficulties will be mastered, and we do not need to be afraid of them. We will have to learn how to control atomic energy without blasting the world out of existence. We will have to learn how to master pollution if we do not want to choke on our filth. It will be a minor question how to keep the field of group psychotherapy free of abuse.

The glory and the despair of being human is to be weak and to have the strength to overcome this weakness. The new assignment of therapy will be to protect people against future shock and to regulate future pull. Without such controls an epidemic of dropouts at all ages can be predicted and suicide, the final form of dropping out of life, will become prevalent.

What the world needs is a utopian vision and the willingness to realize it. The time to do so is now.

Profile of the Group Therapist

Introduction

The study of the therapist as a person is of central importance because group therapy, even more than standard psychoanalysis, is based on the dynamics of interaction of which the therapist is an essential part. He stands in the center of the group process. The literature on psychotherapy often discusses transference and counter-transference and demands that the therapist know himself well enough to be aware of his countertransference and use it as an instrument of understanding.

Psychoanalysis of the therapist is essential but limited in its approach because it does not reach the conflict-free areas of the person. These conflict-free areas become obvious in any group of therapists and can be analyzed there. The therapist's physique, age, sex, cultural background, his sense of values, and his sincerity are all parts of his personality that may never be touched upon in analysis but that play an important role in treatment, especially in group therapy. The therapist must analyze the conflict-free areas of the person and their influence on the group. And he must turn this awareness into an advantage.

Personality traits include many things. Whether the analyst or group therapist is active or passive by nature or training; whether he is inclined to mood swings, from depressive to enthusiastic, from optimistic to pessimistic; whether he has a sense of humor, is witty or dull; whether he shows tolerance or signs of puritanism; whether he is free with tenderness or on the strict side, at ease or overcautious, even tempered or given to fits of impatience or dogmatism; whether he is spontaneous and shows inner freedom or is bound by rigidity—all this has a direct bearing on what is called the therapeutic atmosphere of a group. The therapist's conscious awareness of himself and his impact on people may decide the intensity and the speed with which a working alliance is established and maintained.

10

The Therapist as a Person

A wicked man cannot drive out the Devil.
                    The Gospel of John.

A psychotherapist should be a man for all seasons. He should be reliable; he must invite trust and confidence. In order to do so, he should have trust and confidence in himself, as well as in other people.

He need not be superior in his knowledge, nor even in his intelligence. Any one of his patients may be superior in some respect, but none should be superior in honesty and sincerity. He must be a master of communication, both with himself and with the people he tries to understand. His honesty must extend into the unconscious and for that he needs courage. What a therapist says must be truly felt. How much he says and to whom and when and how he says it, is a question of his style.

The therapist must be a man who has experienced life to the fullest or at least is willing to do so. He may be young or old, but he must have the courage to experience life on many levels; he must know how it feels to be alive. He must have known fear and anxiety, mastery and dependency, and he must not be afraid to love, nor be a stranger to hate.

I also believe that a therapist ought to be a man of reading, since the experience of having lived with the great figures of literature is part of his humanity. The images with which he has to deal are found among friends, lovers, patients colleagues, and enemies; but the models of struggle and integration are found in the characters of great literature, starting perhaps with the Bible. A therapist must have known one woman in love; through her he may know them all.

An analyst should look back on his life style as a proud expression of a lifelong creative effort. He may as well consider himself his own favorite patient – one who has to learn as long as he lives. This thirst for knowledge and for learning belongs, together with honesty and sincerity, to his basic qualifications. They make it possible for him to rely on people and to relate. He does not need to develop a relationship easily and quickly; he may proceed slowly and with care. But the relationships he forms must be deep and based on trust. He will experience disappointment, but he must not become paranoid.

A therapist does not need to be a *Menschen Kenner* (best but incompletely translated as "knower of men") in the practical sense of the word. Therapists often fail sadly in this respect, Freud not being an exception. Although the practical knowledge of men includes the knowledge of man's baseness, a therapist ought to keep his belief in the essential goodness of people, or his work will fail and become an unbearable burden.

The therapist's lifelong learning and his constant creative effort for growth and maturation may single him out from other people, and there is a definite professional trend to isolation, alienation, and detachment. The affection of the people with whom he has worked may mislead the therapist into what has been called "the God Complex." The mature analyst knows this danger and remains skeptical of himself, since he knows he is not quite so bad as he fears he could be and that he is probably not quite so good as he had hoped to be. At all times the therapist should realize better than anybody else that, in the words of Greenson, "the best of us are just good beginners."

The therapist ought to have the courage for "unlimited communication" (Carl Jaspers), which includes the conscious and unconscious. He must be a master in what Franz Alexander called "dynamic reasoning." He must learn how to see people in the here and now and in their

relationship to him but also in their long-term psychological development (their life style), from the beginning to today, with a vague
awareness of tomorrow. His understanding may start with the understanding of a particular person, here and now, but it must extend to
understanding how people become what they are. In this sense, the
therapist is an historian.

The true psychologist must be driven by the wish to understand,
and in that way he is a scientist. At the same time he must be able to
stand the tension of not understanding. Theodor Reik said that it is
better not to understand than to misunderstand. Like a good Quaker,
the therapist must be able to wait for the light to shine, even if he has
to suffer periods of darkness.

Heinz Kohut postulated for the psychoanalyst a "central firmness
and peripheral looseness." This means that the therapist must have a
firm and stable identity. He must know at all times who he is, who he
has been, and where he is going. But he must be proud of his peripheral
sense, by which he perceives people—their affectionate and living
relationship to him and others and their hostility, viciousness, and
ill-will. He ought to be a definite person, a unique individual, but with
an open mind, ready to perceive change and to consider changing.

If the therapist's basic love for psychological truth is all prevailing,
it will protect him from becoming a judge or a policeman. He must be
able to deal with dilemmas and contradictions. He must combine his
lust for discovery with the patience to listen. He must shift from
gaining insight to problem-solving and thinking. He must follow his
patients with a partial but reversible regression; at the same time,
another part of him must remain observing, rational, and integrating.
He must offer himself as a more or less blank screen in order to invite
the development of the transference. He must simultaneously be
human and real enough to establish a working alliance. If he tries to
remain only a blank screen, he will lose his patient. If he offers himself
too loudly as a helper or teammate in the working alliance, the patient
may feel dominated and not understood. It is this bipolarity that makes
the work of the therapist difficult.

The therapist does not need to deny that his interest in people
grows from instinctual sources. During the years of his training and his
work, the trend to understand must become deinstinctualized and
desexualized. Like a surgeon, he must want to penetrate, and like a
physician, he must want to heal. If his original infantile curiosity to

understand is based too much on hostile, invasive penetration, he will endanger his work. When he is too much afraid of the wish to penetrate, he will not go deep enough with his understanding.

The therapist may as well accept his motherliness. He must not try to be a man only. He must accept a partial identification with the mother he wanted to penetrate, to destroy, but also to understand and finally to be. It is the good mother he has to restore within himself.

The therapist does not need to be eloquent, not even erudite or outstandingly logical. He must be able to comprehend, to relate and to communicate.

The therapist has to tolerate many contradictions in himself. He has to be patient and impatient at the same time. He must be able to love and to hate, to be a friend and an opponent to the same person. Only when he does not deny his feelings will the patient be able to trust him. The therapist must be aware of his patient's need for symbiotic fusion with the mother. This need, as Mahler and Guntrip have shown, is the basis for the wish to be understood.

SPONTANEOUS RESPONSIVENESS

The group therapist must be a person of spontaneity and responsiveness. The response must be spontaneous, natural, and direct, but it must be combined with an always ready sense of responsibility.

Perhaps there are advantages for a group therapist in being able and willing to split himself into an observing and an identifying part. The therapist must be able to perform with ease and with grace the rather deep splitting of his person. He always has to remain firmly grounded in his identity; at the same time, he must be able to split off parts of his personality, which he then projects into different members of the group in order to understand them by partial projective identification. He has to perform this splitting process at all times in order to remain simultaneously a participant and an observer, an active member of the group and the central figure – perceiving, responding and interpreting.

The experienced analyst who starts working with groups has to learn the use of spontaneity as a technical device. An analyst in a one-to-one relationship may have more time to wait, to think, to speculate – like a slow-moving chess player. The efficiency of a group therapist is much more dependent on the quick and correct use of his spontaneous responses, growing out of his intuition, empathy, and feeling for the situation. He learns to perceive subliminal cues and to trust his hunches. He acts like the conductor of an orchestra.

A therapist frequently understands a move or a reaction or a therapeutic intervention only after it has taken place. When a therapist works with other therapists as patients in his group, he is often challenged and may be able to formulate only afterward the reasons which prompted him in his spontaneous response. The group therapist depends on his immediate, intuitive, emotional, and honest responses.

The group is a superb educator, supervisor, analyst and therapist. Any therapist who wants to learn from his group is on the right track. As a patient in analysis shows the way he must be treated, so does the group.

TO TRUST AND TO BE TRUSTED

The free use of spontaneity is only possible by a therapist who trusts himself. Since he also must have trust and confidence in the group he must possess the courage and the strength to withstand bad experiences.

The question of such trust leads directly to the central problem of group therapy. A trusting therapist invites trust. Just as a trusting mother gains the confidence of her children, so does she give to her children the basis for their self-confidence. Only the well-mothered infant, as Winnicott said, develops that kind of basic trust which is necessary for mental health in later life. Erikson and Guntrip have shown that nobody can develop this basic trust by himself. A person can develop everything else in the process of individuation, but the basic trust has to be started with the experience of the mother–infant symbiosis. Fairbairn has shown this convincingly. If this relationship is traumatized or even destroyed, it is an almost hopeless assignment to restore it in treatment.

A well-conducted group may be capable of inviting such basic trust and self-reliance to develop. At least it can be developed from cautious beginnings in the group better than in a one-to-one relationship.

The analyst may be astounded to find that members of a group begin to trust the group more than they trust the therapist alone. It is this trust that the therapist must be able to invite, handle, and finally, deserve. The group therapist must know how to develop and protect the trust of the group – primarily to the group and secondarily to himself, as the parental and central figure.

The therapist's spontaneity, his responsiveness, his ability for temporary projective identifications are the tools of his trade. They determine the efficiency of the therapeutic group process. If the group therapist is like the conductor of an orchestra, an analyst is more like a critic who sits in the audience and occasionally gets up, stops the concert, makes a remark, and sits down again to listen. He does not conduct. He limits himself more or less to interpretations. The group therapist has to respond first and interpret later. Only a therapist who has learned to trust the different aspects of his countertransference is equipped to work well in groups.

THE DIFFERENCE BETWEEN ACTOR AND PERFORMER

When I once asked Franz Alexander a technical question of therapy he shocked me with his answer, "The success of such technique depends entirely on how good an actor you are." I never had considered myself an actor and never considered being or becoming one since. I realized much later the difference between an actor and a performer. An actor acts as if he were somebody else while a performer performs a real task and chooses to do it in front of an audience and in a way that can be observed and understood by others.

A conductor communicates with the language of his body what he wants the orchestra to do. He shows what he does, but what he does is real and not pretended. He performs his duty. An actor would behave as if he were conducting. When I am angry in the therapeutic situation, I allow myself to feel my anger. I use my judgment to decide how much anger to show and when and in what form. The basic emotion must be honestly and truly felt, while the expression of this emotion will be a part of the therapist's skill or his "performance."

I once watched a building being torn down by people working with monstrous machines. Quite a number of sidewalk superintendents were gathered to watch, and I joined them. There was one man who ran his enormous machine with strength, power, and pride. He was doing his work and at the same time he did it in a way that was easily spotted, singled out, and applauded. He was not an actor, he was a performer. He did what had to be done in a way that it became visible and understandable.

There is a great difference between an actor who acts the role of a general and a general who performs his duties so that his men can see what he does and history may judge him. The trust of the group is partly based on seeing the therapist in his performance.

In one of my groups a young actor occasionally could not resist the temptation to dramatize what he was feeling. When he was depressed he showed it all over the place; and when he was angry he acted almost frightening. When we caught on that he was acting the whole group set to the task of doubting him until he showed what he was feeling without dramatizing it. Through these lessons, he became a more honest man and a better actor on the stage.

FIRM IDENTITY AND OPEN MINDEDNESS

The central firmness of the group therapist allows him to be recognized as what he is. The group wants to know whom they are trusting. The group's trust is not based entirely upon an anonymous screen; in addition to being a transference figure, he is also a real person. He is the central figure, symbolizing the parent in all the various shades of transference. His open mind (or his peripheral looseness) toward the group allows him to perform his duties by being father to one, mother to all, affectionate friend to somebody who needs one, disciplinarian to somebody who may at that time be working on problems of authority. He must not get lost in the pitiful spectacle of a multiple personality. His central firmness or ego identity will protect him against that. He must remain what he is—he, himself, and nobody else.

Naturally this firmness must be combined with his constant readiness to learn, to change, to develop, and to grow. The therapist is not a patient in the group, but just as a good parent allows the members of his family to recognize him in strength and in weakness, so the good therapist—more than the analyst—may show himself as a real person.

Doing so invites the members of the group-family to become independent and to avoid the danger of regressive infantilization, which is such danger in an ill-conducted psychoanalysis.

A SENSE OF HUMOR

A sense of humor can help the group therapist to keep the group from unnecessary infantilization. It counteracts the tendency to idealize him as an omniscient and omnipotent parental figure. A man with a sense of humor invites the group to look at him realistically and to correct the transference exaggerations.

The therapist's sense of humor reassures the group and allows the patients to pierce the therapist's character defenses since obviously he can take it and even laugh about himself with the group. It is important for the group to see in the therapist a transference figure *and* a real person. No therapist can remain a blank screen within a group.

The therapist has to be on guard with his wit and his fondness for the wisecrack and the sharply pointed and often painfully penetrating remark. Such remarks show his incompletely resolved ambivalence and perhaps some sadistic traits, which would have no place among the tools of a therapist. He may employ his wit occasionally to counteract the trend to hero worship.

TO ERR IS HUMAN – EVEN FOR A THERAPIST

The group therapist may make mistakes: he is expected and allowed to do so. His honesty makes it possible for him to accept the correction of his mistake by the group, the way the head of a family would listen to others in a family council. The therapist does not lose his position by admitting to a mistake. On the contrary, his central position may be confirmed.

I certainly do not like to confess to having made a mistake; however, I let my patients feel that I respect them, and that I take them seriously and consider what they say as meaningful. If a patient calls me an s.o.b., I consider the remark in the first place a sign of the patient's negative transference, but there is always a nagging suspicion in me that I may have done something that rightfully caused the patient to react with bitterness.

If an entire group unanimously stands up in censuring me, I am sure that I have misjudged the situation. But even then there are exceptions. I have been in situations where I felt and actually was misunderstood by everybody. These are the moments when the therapist may retreat into a silently waiting attitude. A group therapist should always be ready to respond quickly but slow to retaliate.

11

The Therapist as a Patient

A man who accepts his patienthood has a good chance to become a good therapist. Every physician should learn how to use the experience of being sick to become a better physician. As a rule, however, the medical man is a poor patient, and that is nothing to be proud of. The situation is the same in the development of a group psychotherapist. Psychoanalysis teaches insight and understanding, but group psychotherapy offers therapy to the therapist.

When a physician consults another physician because he is sick, he inevitably says to his colleague: "I want you to treat me like any other patient." To which the consulted colleague is honor-bound to answer: "That is my intention. I would not do it otherwise." And they both promptly relate to each other like two colleagues discussing a most interesting third person. The results may be tragic in the case of serious illness.

It is true that the therapist has to become a patient. The question is how to accomplish it. The physician is different from the average patient who knows little about his body and nothing about the function of his inner organs. The neurotic patient knows little about his unconscious while the therapist knows much, even when he tries to be a patient and feels sick like one.

The physician in medical treatment and the therapist in training have to learn how to split themselves into two parts – one remaining a therapist and joining his colleague as cotherapist, another becoming a patient. This splitting makes the working alliance in training and therapy different from other treatment situations. If not handled correctly, it seriously limits the therapeutic efficacy of the training analysis. The therapist in training or therapy has to learn how to perform such a split, and the teacher has to facilitate it. If the teacher accepts his therapist-students only as students, they will never become patients, since they want to become what the training analyst is, an accomplished therapist. Training will become an initiation ritual. To be effective training must combine the therapeutic alliance with a learning experience.

THE ANALYTIC GROUP EXPERIENCE

It has been said that young psychiatrists talk about their cases, established psychiatrists talk about money, and senior analysts talk about themselves. After forty-eight years of work in psychiatry and in psychoanalysis, I am presumably ready for the third stage. Accordingly, I would like to mention the reasons why I have turned to group therapy; this turn is a result of continued introspection and examination of my work as a psychotherapist and as an instructor of psychotherapists.

A senior colleague once confessed with some embarrassment to another great teacher of psychoanalysis that he felt fed up with supervision because for many years he felt as if he had been teaching little children to spell "cat" and they still did not know how. This is about what happened to my attitude toward psychoanalytic training in general.

By contrast, I recently had the chance to observe the development of six young resident-psychiatrists. I saw them through almost three years of twice weekly group sessions, and it was my impression that they learned a great deal – perhaps as much as they would have learned during the same time in individual psychoanalysis. They gained understanding of themselves and insight into each other and their interaction, both conscious and unconscious. This learning was deepened by interpretation and by the emotional experience of honest and free response to each other. They experienced their relationship to the therapist as a central figure more or less as they would have done in the one-to-one relationship of psychoanalysis. They also experienced their relationship to each other, thus including peer relationships in the learning situation.

In spite of my good experience with group therapy in the training of resident psychiatrists, I still recommend previous standard analysis as a foundation for all psychological training.

This group of young doctors differed greatly from a group of experienced analysts who formed another group which I studied for several years as their therapist. All had undergone long, repeated, therapeutic and didactic analyses before, during, and after their training. With growing analytic sophistication, they all realized that the one-to-one relationship was not enough to give them a satisfying and lasting therapeutic experience. They all had learned to master the one-to-one relationship, frequently in the service of their resistance. They had learned to handle and manage their different analysts and to stop further progress effectively where they wanted it to stop. The change from analytic loneliness to the group experience and peer relationship continued and then deepened the analytic process they had started in their analyses and continued in their work as psychoanalysts.

One analyst is not enough in the terminal stage of an analysis for a therapist. Repeated analysis by different analysts had been recommended and tried, by Lawrence Kubie (1968) for example. Analysts learn how to deal with their own analysts, how to disarm the analytic process, and how to establish a mutual adjustment. Another analyst is not the solution to this phenomenon. Equally unsatisfactory is an ever longer training analysis. Neither is a friend able to continue the analysis of an analyst where his training left off. In such a friendship there is too much affection, too much relaxation, too little freely expressed emotion, and not enough working through of the transference.

A new transference situation is needed, and this is provided by the one-of-us relationship in the group. The transference of peers to each other and to the group as a mother image is needed in order to analyze the analyst within the family transference. Most analysts growing older in their profession lose the trust, confidence, and faith in their colleagues that they had when they started as young men and accepted an analytic working relationship to older training analysts. As they grow older, a certain therapeutic skepticism takes hold of them. In the one-to-one relationship of standard analysis this skepticism becomes even stronger. It is easier to activate confidence and trust in a group than in an individual setting.

A middle-aged analyst came to me once, because I had seen him through a part of his analytic training many years previously. The analyst was in one of those depressions significant for aging analysts: he felt isolated, alienated, bored, skeptical, disappointed, almost cynical. I spent some time with him and then invited him to join one of my groups. This one was reserved for analysts only, since they close ranks in defense of psychoanalysis when outsiders are present. Also their style of free-associative communication is sometimes frightening or unintelligible to the uninitiated. This middle-aged analyst joined the group with the usual reservation and resistance; then at the first meeting he surprised me by telling two symbolic stories from his childhood that highlighted his entire life development. After the session, I did not want to confess outright that these stories were new to me and so I said diplomatically: "You know, we never fully analyzed the meaning of those two significant stories while you were in analysis." The younger analyst said bluntly: "Because I never told them to you." An association too revealing to be told to the parental image of the analyst was easily told as an introduction and presentation to his peers.

Two additional observations may help to explain why the analytic group experience is of special therapeutic and learning importance for the analyst as well as for the later group therapist. These observations relate to conflict-free areas and negative transference.

CONFLICT-FREE PERSONALITY TRENDS

Conflict free personality trends are areas of the therapist's ego structure which are important in his work and in his relationship to people but hardly ever show up in the analysis and therefore cannot be analyzed. The reason for this feeling of analysis is the fact that they are conflict free and therefore cause no suffering. It is also my observation that these important features cannot be analyzed when they become known in supervision. I prefer therefore a consistent and careful therapy in the group for the therapist, because there these areas will show in relationship to the therapist's peers. These areas involve such things as the distribution and combination of activity and passivity; maleness and femaleness; outer-directedness and inner-directedness; enthusiasm, sobriety, or indifference; masochistic and sadistic trends; sensitive and insensitive social consciousness; tolerance and intolerance; affectionate and hostile trends; spontaneity and intellectualization; patience and impatience; and personal tempo.

THE ANALYSIS OF NEGATIVE TRANSFERENCE IN THE TRAINING SITUATION

The transference to the training analyst is by design a transference to a parental figure with realistic authority. Since the student-therapist wants to become like his analyst, he submits to him and seems to do so willingly. Secretly, however, and out of reach, he harbors a rebellion which will be expressed only later. In the analytic group situation, where the peer relationship prevails, this repressed and unanalyzed rebelliousness comes to the surface of consciousness and can be analyzed.

Analysts have failed to deal with this rebelliousness in the therapy that is an essential part of training. Clinical evidence of this failure is provided by many analysts and is apparent in the pathology of their behavior in their societies and institutes; it is apparent in their relationship to colleagues and last but not least in their family life. Since this hostility is unanalyzed, it is also continued from one generation to the next.

The problem of negative transference and hostility in training analysis has remained a central, controversial issue. Since the patient, in his desire to be like his analyst, postpones his rebellion and much of the negative transference until he is through with his training, it usually hits him with great force and leads to internal personal problems and to manifest problems in interaction with his colleagues. The analyst carries his unresolved hostility into the family of analysts.

The problem of the analysis of negative transference is also a countertransference problem. Fathers want to be loved by their student-sons who, after all, represent the future. Therefore, analysts tend to relate differently to their training candidates in action, behavior, and interpretation than they do to most of their other patients.

Lawrence Kubie has confessed that in his opinion the transference neurosis is never really dissolved in a training analysis. As a remedy, he asks for a real relationship in the form of a controlled, low-intensity friendship after the formal analysis. He also suggests a change of analyst during the terminal stage of training. The new analyst should offer insight into the residual transference to the first analyst.

THE THERAPIST'S FAMILY ROMANCE AND THE ANALYTIC GROUP EXPERIENCE

The analytic group experience offers decisive help in the final resolution of negative transference relationships. The transference in the group situation is not simply a continuation of the infantile neurosis. The group offers a reenactment of the family neurosis. The group invites freer expression of hostility than in the one-to-one relationship. A young man will have difficulty attacking an older man who may represent a professional ideal. An older man has learned from experience to be cautious with a younger colleague. In a therapeutic group, these trends are much less intense, less focussed, and more easily expressed, interpreted, and integrated.

The group members can freely dish out hostility, and the therapist can freely respond to it. The whole atmosphere of a well-conducted group is much freer than the analytic atmosphere.

Group members, knowing that their peers share their feelings, are encouraged by the fact that they will not be isolated in their hostility and guilt. The central figure, on the other hand, is much more at ease to accept hostility since he knows that rarely will the entire group join in hostile rebellion. The central figure may much more freely express his counterhostility in a group, since he can trust the group to react to him, and keep him from becoming destructive or intimidating.

The student body of an analytic training institute forms a peer-group. But this family remains in an unconsciously motivated transference situation and, therefore, is in need of being analyzed. This analysis can best be done in the family transference setting of group psychotherapy.

SOME SPECIFIC FEATURES OF DIDACTIC
GROUPS

Young therapists are inclined to use intellectualization as a form of resistance. An often heard phrase in a didactic group is: "We all talk like a bunch of smart professionals." However, the avoidance of intellectualization after it has been repeatedly called by that term may lead to a new form of resistance. Insights are resolutely rejected because they may sound "too intellectual."

Therapists in a group have to learn how to replace questions with associative responses. In the first stage of group formation, professional members try to confirm their impressions and planned interpretations by fishing for clinical evidence. They soon realize that their spontaneous response is more important and often contains the proper interpretation, or leads to it. They then develop the courage to be spontaneous and overcome the handicap imposed by being a medical man who is suspicious of spontaneity and who has been trained to filter his responses carefully.

Work in groups of psychiatrists or analysts is tough for the central figure. Whether experienced or inexperienced, a group of colleagues will recognize the therapist's weak spots. They use their therapeutic skill to put their collective finger where it hurts most and the narcissistic therapist may feel in need of a hiding place. If he is open, responsive, and ready to learn, he will succeed—as does a father who accepts democracy and freedom in his family.

The conduct of a training group for therapists is excellent postgraduate training for the central figure as well as for the members of the group. The therapist has to perform in the presence of six or eight alert and specially trained critics. At times the experience amounts to something like a special board examination. Anyone who passes such a test has received a baptism of fire. The analyst who has difficulty in allowing himself to feel his hostility or his need for tenderness benefits the most. He can learn how to be more free, spontaneous, and responsive. The same group that exposes him also protects him until he finds his way to an attitude appropriate for him. The psychoanalyst fulfills his need for intimacy in the one-to-one relationship; in the group he may satisfy his need for participation in the growth and maturation of a family.

When working in groups, an analyst's narcissism takes a severe blow. When he steps out of his professional isolation, he sees that he is not the only good therapist. But he also realizes that he is not making many more mistakes than his colleagues. After the group experience, a new, more humble and realistic attitude replaces his narcissism and makes him a better therapist.

THE THERAPIST'S MARRIAGE

A great deal of a therapist's future depends on his marriage, his wife, and his children. I occasionally tell my students how much they can learn outside the seminars, at home, from and in their families. The analyst should never be a therapist in his own family; there he should act and react, not analyze. Group psychotherapy seems especially suited for therapists' spouses because they have to learn that nobody can be a therapist in his own family, even if he is an expert on other families.

Group work with therapists' wives brings them relief from the burden of secrecy. The partner in an analyst's marriage often feels left out of an important part of her husband's life. In the group, she is introduced into his work, its pleasure and pain, its frustration and its hope.

One of the outstanding problems a therapist has to face is what David Morgan called the Mother Superior complex. The therapist's need to be Mother Superior at home can be well analyzed in a group. This need is frequently neglected in individual analyses, since it is often conflict-free and is an integral part of our attitude of healing. Many analysts and perhaps all physicians have an unconscious need to show their wives that women are bad mothers and that doctors would be much better mothers if given a free hand. The doctor's Mother Superior complex leads him to unfair competition at home, causing heart-breaking trouble and frequently leading to a sadomasochistic, malignant acting out, which can be aggravated by quick and unannounced role reversals. The children pay the price for the parents' competitiveness.

Any woman so foolish as to marry a physician who is, in addition, a therapist, must gain insight into her husband's tendency not to project his own feminine trends onto her but to keep them jealously embedded in his own behavior. In this respect the therapist strays specifically from the normal course of heterosexual love. The therapist's wife has to learn how to invite her husband to trust her and to love his feminine tendencies not in himself but in her. The other women in the group of therapists often restore a woman's strength and belief in her own femininity, which has been endangered by a therapist-husband's competitiveness. A therapist at home can be dangerous when he "gaslights" his wife, as a group of wives called it. It means to drive somebody slowly, consistently, deliberately, and occasionally successfully into madness by skillfully undermining her self-confidence and identity as a mother, wife, and woman. The therapist's wife should never forget a warning of David Morgan's: "For better or worse we are stuck with our profession, even more than with our families." A therapist may divorce his wife, but never his profession.

A WIFE'S REACTION TO HER
HUSBAND'S THERAPEUTIC MOTHERLINESS

Martha preferred to be in her own group while her husband, a psychotherapist, joined another group. She complained bitterly about feeling neglected by her hardworking husband. She was angered out of all proportion about his patients who did not pay. To repeat the bills at the end of the month caused bitter, acrimonious, and fruitless fights. If she rented her husband out to others, she wanted at least to receive financial rewards.

It was the group's and my impression that the woman could not get herself to say simply and directly to her husband: "You don't love me any more, you neglect me and your own family, you love your patients, your groups, your therapeutic family, your sick children. The proof of your love for them is in your neglecting the economic basis of your business. You do not insist on being properly paid because only prostitutes and pimps get paid for love." Behind this woman's unrealistic rage was her great suspicion and jealousy and frustration about the fact that she wanted to love her husband who in turn loved his work more than he loved her. This is a most frequently found trouble in the marriage of a therapist. It is equally often not realized and therefore not directly accessible to change.

The husband was not acting like an analyst at home but like a husband who felt terribly misunderstood and unappreciated. He worked so hard and with so much devotion, and his wife did not appreciate his sacrifice but demanded her share of him. He could prove that more than 90 percent of his bills were eventually paid. There are always some people who wait, delay, and sometimes never pay.

Women do not always realize that the men they love respond only with partial love; the other part goes into their work and into the affection for their sick "children," or patients. To see this is a good beginning to saving such a marriage, but it is not the final answer. Men have to learn not to come home tired but unbowed from a fictitious battle for existence, expecting the special consideration, love, and nursing due a hero. They must realize that they have indulged in their favorite activity. They do not need to feel guilty but must keep within limits which leave enough of energy for wives and families.

Women will always continue to fight for their husbands, but they will do it with less viciousness and with more patience when the situation is understood. The chances are they will win – not in that the men lose interest in their work, but in that they find the right way to satisfy their own needs for being good mothers both in the office and at home and finally even to their wives. Women need a long time to realize that we are more deeply rooted in our profession than in our marriage. It takes a great, good, and strong woman to accept this fact, within reasonable limits. It is not easy to be married to a therapist and only the innocent and the dreamer will feel envious of the fate of a therapist's wife. She as a rule is the last one to be understood by her loving therapist husband.

THE PHYSICIAN'S TRIUMPH OVER THE BIOLOGICAL MOTHER

The therapist's motherliness or his maternal identification can be seen in a peculiar symptom which as a rule remains within the limits of a physician's normal pathology. I have often wondered what the dynamics are of a slight manic episode observable in busy medical men. The physician with depressive trends or a melancholic character undergoes a personality change the moment he enters his office and sees the waiting patients, impatient nurses, piled-up mail, the detail men trying to sell him drugs he never knew existed, and hears the telephone ringing with demands, worries, and emergencies. His behavior changes as if an electric light had been turned on and the darkness had vanished. A similar change can be seen in a surgeon operating or helping to deliver a baby, or in a psychiatrist calming a schizophrenic in a catatonic excitement.

I consider all these slight or outspoken stages of elation as the physician's triumph over the bad mother. She had made her children sick or defective and he, the physician, is the healer. I am the better mother, the Mater Superior, the mother of the Gods. The physician's triumph is the triumph over the biological mother.

THE THERAPIST'S MENTAL HEALTH

The therapist does not need to be a paragon of mental health in order to be a good therapist. He can perform well in the face of his own anxiety. He can proceed efficiently with such psychosomatic conversions as high blood pressure, migraine, or a gastric ulcer. It is preferable for a therapist to overcome his symptoms, and he sometimes does. The analysis and correction of conflict-free areas takes time and the therapist may work well before his own therapy is completed.

I have doubts about paranoid trends in a group therapist, since a suspicious and distrustful therapist may communicate his suspicions in a way that does not benefit the group process. A therapist who has passed through a psychotic episode may do well to disqualify himself for his own and his patients' sake, even if he sometimes shows a remarkable understanding of the sickest patients. This is not the understanding of a therapist any more but the understanding of a fellow sufferer for his brother. It may lead to a kind of understanding which will only rarely lead to effective therapeutic intervention.

There are, however, many exceptions. A slight and perhaps even chronic depressive position may be a qualification for a therapist. In the face of so much suffering, a sensitive person almost must become slightly depressed. It is a kind of existential despair, a way of being human, an acknowledgment of our impossible profession. It does not interfere with the therapist's functioning. It may give him that kind of maturity a child expects from his parents.

The group therapist may be a man who knows anxiety and fear as well as depression and despair. In the therapeutic alliance with his patients, he must not fear his fears.

12

Awareness and Use of Countertransference

The proper use of the therapist's countertransference nourishes and develops different aspects of the multiple transference situation in the group. With his central identity, he is able to offer himself as a screen for different projections. He is guided by his knowledge of multileveled and multichanneled communication.

The peer transference situation in the group-family imposes a demand on the therapist that is less obvious in individual treatment. The analyst has no competition; the group therapist is surrounded by all the members of the group whose responses are next in importance to his own interpretation. The group therapist should not fight with the members of the group for dominance by narcissistically displaying his brilliance or by showing his superiority in other ways.

The group therapist must realize that the peer relationship is an effective way to exercise therapeutic pressure. He should be able to handle this relationship without envy and interference by inviting it and protecting it. A jealous parent is not a good parent.

The analyst in the analytic situation almost invites resistance: the patient feels at times as if he must defend his sickness against the father who wants to eliminate it. The peer relationship in the group situation is less threatening and invites cooperative effort.

The therapist's and the group's maternal attitude facilitates the patient's experience of nursing, weaning and individuation. It is a peculiar paradox that people have an excellent opportunity for individuation while working interdependently in groups. Dissolving the mother–infant symbiosis may amount to an experience of rebirth in the group.

A good mother has to learn that a child is a "going concern," in Winnicott's words, and the good therapist, as mother, must learn how to trust the group, just as he would a child who is developing his own mastery. Trust in the well-mothered child is rewarded by the child's self-confidence. This is a good model for the therapist of the progress of a well-conducted group.

INNER VISUALIZATION AS A HELP TO UNDERSTANDING

Ross and Kapp (1962) suggested that the therapist use inner visualization to catch his own unconscious reaction to the free-associative dialogue with the patient. This inner visualization, or view with the third eye, helps the therapist find understanding first in visual and symbolic form and then in verbal formulation.

I have used this approach for many years without being fully aware of it. Only lately have I developed it into a technical tool that has grown to characterize my style of empathy – one especially helpful in group work. Here is a description of this inner visualization:

A slightly depressed patient told the group about a dream. He took a walk with his daughter, crossed a river, and admired the beautiful landscape.

I was still busy in my mind with the last interaction between some group members and was not yet willing to follow the dream, and so it did not speak to me. When I turned into myself to perceive the visual images that appeared on my inner screen while listening, I saw hieroglyphics cast on the walls of an Egyptian tomb; then appeared the sarcophagus, from which the body of the Pharaoh had been removed to show an exquisitely painted picture of the goddess of death with outstretched arms, ready to receive her Pharaoh, her son, brother and lover. From there it was only a question of how to formulate the insight in order to show the patient his preoccupation with death.

Special beauty in dreams generally signifies the beauty of the peace one hopes to find after death. Later, returning to the dream, it could be seen that the longing for death is a hope for the final reunion with the powerful, beautiful, and eternally waiting mother. Every group at some time or other has to deal with the problems of death and dying, loss, mourning, and grief.

THE SPECIAL CASE OF SPLIT TRANSFERENCE

Occasionally a colleague refers a patient in analysis with him for group therapy with me. The referring analyst hopes that this combination of analysis and group experience may stimulate progress in the patient, which it often does.

I find these patients interesting to work with, and on the basis of my experience, I recommend group experience for everyone undergoing analysis, but especially for a future therapist. There is, however, a certain danger of the transference being split between the analyst and the group therapist. I saw a therapist in training who gladly accepted the recommendation to join one of my groups and immediately split his transference – attaching his negative and hostile feelings to his analyst, who had referred him and thus rejected him, and forming a positive, loving transference to me as the group therapist who had accepted him and invited him into "my family." When the referring analyst, in this case a friend of mine, trusts me, then the situation can be worked out without difficulties. If the analyst is not a trusting friend, it would be a mistake to accept the patient in the first place. With time, patience and repeated interpretation the split transference can be analyzed.

POSITIVE COUNTERTRANSFERENCE IN THE ANALYTIC TRAINING SITUATION

Therapists training colleagues must be aware of their affection which we have for the younger colleague, our brother and son, future and hope.

Two examples are presented in which a realistic factor led to the correction of such a positive countertransference.

In one group, there was a young doctor whom I definitely favored. I liked the way he expressed his understanding, his truly brother-like relationship to his group mates, and his attitude of restrained respect toward me. Another young man in another group was similarly favored for a while, and the group noticed it before he himself reacted to it. Only then did I realize that both men shared the first name of my son. I caught myself in a benevolent acting out of positive countertransference feelings which could then be handled gracefully.

THE THERAPIST'S MOTHERLINESS IN THE NEGATIVE COUNTERTRANSFERENCE

I am fully aware that my groups represent families to me, with whom I live, with whom I enjoy life, and with whom I suffer through crises. I feel consciously that I am trying to be a good father-mother. I know that being a father involves providing the motherliness Sigmund Freud displayed in his relationship to the early group of analytic pioneers. The main attribute of a good mother is her unselfishness. She does not look out for her own benefit but for that of her children. She may do this silently and limit herself to watching; she may offer her advice when asked; and she may show her caring by understanding her maturing children.

The analytic mother or "parent" must have the inner strength to stand up against all sorts of negative feelings. Without this strength the therapist would be practically valueless. Love alone is not enough, neither for a mother nor for an analytic parent.

After I had worked with groups for a number of years I studied my records in order to determine the type of people who dropped out of treatment. I found to my surprise several younger colleagues among these dropouts. I had completely forgotten about them when I started my research project. They were determined to murder the father and by eliminating themselves from the group they had symbolically murdered me. Looking back at the transference–countertransference situation, I do not believe that any other outcome was possible.

Among the dropouts I found three women who were so unpleasant and who tried to be so domineering and controlling that in trying to confront them with their behavior, I lost them and they left the group in indignation. They knew everything best and they handed out bits of wisdom which always sounded as if they found their philosophy in Chinese fortune cookies.

I got unreasonably irritated and annoyed with them, trying to show them that this is not the way to learn in a group. I tried to confront them with their behavior, hoping that they would see that such confrontation was something they had avoided in their previous analysis. I hoped to establish the therapeutic alliance with one part of their personality in order to help me in the fight against the other, unacceptable part. This hope was in vain and these patients were lost. I realized too late that what I was fighting most was my fear that these women would take my family and represent a disciplinary and controlling bad mother. I defended my children too fiercely against the threat of this bad mother.

I have learned to spot would-be applicants for the place of bad mother in the group. I have learned to interpret this specific transference–countertransference development and dropouts of this sort happen less often. There are naturally always people who insist on alarming the therapist with their destructive impulses against the group family, but I react to them in a much more appropriate way, by interpreting their behavior rather than reacting to it.

THE DISAPPOINTED AND THE HURT THERAPIST

I am surprised that I have not yet developed enough callousness to protect myself against sometimes being hurt, annoyed, and disappointed by my patients.

Freud once said in a letter to Max Eitingon that we could help our patients more if we would "take our skin to market for them," which means to risk our vulnerabilities and go all out for them. I often feel that active therapy is more dangerous for the therapist than it is for the patient. If we invest too much in our patients we will get hurt eventually.

I have learned to stand the onslaught of hostility, or negative transference, without undue stress. It took me a little longer to obtain the same equanimity with hostile colleagues to whom I was inclined to feel as toward a younger brother or even a son.

The worst antagonism is activated when I see my group family endangered by somebody who, with furious determination, assumes the role of a bad mother and is on the way to destroying the therapeutic group process.

It is equally disappointing for a therapist to have placed trust and confidence in somebody only to see later that this trust was misplaced. I have always tried not to be hardened by bad experiences and not to lose trust and faith in human nature. Without this faith we may avoid some pain for ourselves, but a protective, defensive, suspicious and too cautious therapist is not a good one.

I am still willing to take risks on my own, but never with my patients' welfare. I can handle my hurt, but I do not feel entitled to expose the group to eventual damage.

THE THERAPIST'S REACTION TO THE GROUP
AFTER HOURS

Only a few times have I joined social activities of the group outside of the session in my office. Once after a late group had left my office, I stopped into a neighborhood cafeteria for something to eat. I was vaguely aware that there was hardly anybody sitting in the cafeteria but that a group of perhaps six or eight people was standing where the food was distributed. Everybody stood back letting me go through, and I wondered whether I now appeared so old that I commanded the respect of people standing in line. When I sat down and started to eat, I was again aware that other people clustered around me. I looked up and recognized that I was surrounded by my group who were looking at me in disbelief that I would not see them.

Another time I knew that some members of different groups went to dinner in a certain restaurant, and since I wished to change an appointment with the wife of one member, I went there to make the change and spend a few minutes with the group at dinner. On such occasions it is most natural for me to behave like a quiet, unobtrusive, tired but outright friendly and benign paternal friend. Through many years as a training analyst who regularly has academic contacts with his younger colleagues in analysis, I had learned that this attitude is the easiest for me as well as for my patients. It causes the least amount of transference reactions.

The experience was different when the wife of a group member who had participated in the group of couples for a number of years became pregnant, as many women do when they begin to accept their femininity. I had told her that when the child was born I would come for "the adoration of the baby." The course of the pregnancy was undisturbed, the delivery was not complicated, and a lovely little baby girl was born. When three months had passed, I accepted an invitation by the husband who was still attending my group. I suspected the whole group would come a little later after my arrival and that was what happened. My wife felt that she was on approval and assumed her role with amused motherliness. She took care of the baby, was friendly to everybody, and it was a pleasure to watch her as a kind of grandmother to the baby and to the group.

There were many different reactions in the group on this occasion. I was aware of one of the women, who, in her erotized transference to me, felt more than ever left out and disappointed. We took that up in our next group session.

There was another woman who worked her way in between me and everybody else and tried to monopolize me. She was the only one to abuse the occasion and who tried to change the conversation into a therapeutic interaction. There was one woman I knew to be unrelated, but to see her fear of human contact in such social situations was a shocking and informative experience for me.

Another observation at the party showed me that the therapeutic situation is always limited and observations made outside of it can sometimes be helpful if brought back into the therapeutic situation. In this case it was, for instance, new and impressive for me to observe that two couples were astonishingly stingy in their contribution to the party's expenses on food. This observation could later be introduced into the course of therapy and could be utilized for insight and eventual change.

On all such occasions, rare as they are, I feel free to register observations and bring them back to the group sessions for discussion and interpretations.

My general impression of such outside contacts with group members confirms an opinion I have had for many years. A therapist may have certain illusions about the people he works with. This is, to a certain extent, equally true for the group of patients. Contact outside the group sometimes verifies these illusions and at other times destroys them.

The therapist learns about his patients and the patients about their therapist, which aids in the final solution of transference and countertransference reactions. There is no reason to avoid contact as there is no good reason to seek it. The family also benefits from occasional outside contact among the group members without the parental authority present.

13

In Quest of a Cotherapist

I have never worked in my office with a cotherapist. I have two groups made up of psychiatrists only, and in addition have one, two and sometimes three psychiatrists in each of my other groups. Under these circumstances, I neither need nor wish for a cotherapist.

I noticed, however, that often one of the group, not necessarily a colleague, unofficially plays the role of cotherapist; sometimes it remains unknown to himself and even to me and sometimes it is acknowledged. Without any manipulation or management the function of a cotherapist passes from one member to another. When I am engaged with one member of the group or with the entire group, then it may just happen that somebody looks at our interaction and may criticize me, analyze my behavior, or contribute by preparing, deepening, or reformulating my interpretation or our interaction. In this way almost every member of any group may be my cotherapist for awhile.

A special situation arises when some of my colleagues in the groups gang up on me, often not fully aware of what they are doing. This is as a rule a hostile form of resistance and has to be interpreted as such. If the entire group turns against me I know I have made a mistake. I then listen, wait, locate my mistake, and analyze the motives for it. I may or may not let the group know what I was thinking. This depends upon the needs and maturity of the group.

There are several points which should be mentioned in any discussion of cotherapists. I always warn my colleagues that under no circumstances should they conduct a marathon meeting without a cotherapist. The arrangement for a cotherapist during a time extended session is a necessity. In predominantly adolescent groups, it is also advisable to have a team of two therapists at hand. This practice follows logically from the dynamics of such groups. When conducting large daily hospital groups, arrangements should be made to have members of the medical staff present who can act as a team of cotherapists.

A special cotherapist situation exists when I am called as a consultant. I do not limit myself to listening to the therapist report about the group. I always insist when the time comes to participate as a consultant in a group with the colleague who asked for the consultation. Only then do I feel that I have any help to offer.

Cotherapists are rarely equals according to my observations. One may be dominant, the other may be the assistant. They may reverse roles by arrangement or spontaneously. One therapist may submerge into interaction, the other may remain observant. A kind of mother-father team may develop, which is of special advantage in family groups including adolescents. It helps to bring a corrective family experience to life.

THE GRUESOME DREAM OF A FRUSTRATED COTHERAPIST

A therapist in group therapy reported the following dream. "I walked through a park and looked down at a rushing little brook, forming to the right side a kind of pool framed by big rocks. Once more I take the same walk and the dream is repeated but now with my wife and my son, age perhaps six. The boy climbs down to the creek to inspect a cave. I decide to look into the cave myself and I go around the rocks, try to enter from the back and pass a wrecked two-seater car. When I enter the cave it is filled with the naked bodies of bloody and murdered children. Directly at my feet is the body of a grown-up man who looks up at me and asks, "Is the murderer still there?" We both walk back to the car and there sleeps the killer. We go back to the cave and I now try to leave in the other direction where it opens to the pond and wake up."

The dreamer continued, "I told the dream three times to myself and have no idea what it means. The cave looked like a body in operation, after acupuncture. The scene was also reminiscent of a cage in a zoo in which bears are kept, or a movie set. It was bloody like the Tate murder case.

"Later while reading an essay on technology which kept my conscious mind concentrated on a topic far removed from anything personal, the dream became suddenly clear to me. It started with my awareness that in the dream I was not shocked by the bloody mess. The murders were not really murders. They were just men 'sleeping at the wheel' and I thought of my great disappointment about my group work in the hospital where everybody sits around in an enormous circle of fifty, leaving an empty spaced fringed by the thin line of people. I referred to this empty space as 'the burial ground of our dead mothers.'

"I see now the pond and the little stream as the dead mother and her dead, unborn fetus-like children. The murderer is my cotherapist who has murdered my good relationship to my patients. He has murdered the project about which I was so enthusiastic. Now the many sick people, all the members of the group, have died."

EVERYONE IS A THERAPIST

I found that almost everybody is a natural therapist. Women may have an edge on men because they find it easier to accept their intuition while the men always look for facts or evidence and are musclebound by reality.

The entire group is a sensitive, thoughtful, and understanding therapist. The most dramatic example of this occurred when I was working as a group therapist in the United States Army. The group was a large one—perhaps forty or forty-five soldiers returning from combat duty. There was one sergeant who with great emotion described the story of his paralyzed right arm and hand. He had been advancing with his troops against a Japanese bunker blocking the road. A number of units had sidestepped it, but his unit was ordered to eliminate the resistance of that fortification. It turned out to be a more formidable assignment than originally assumed. While his soldiers were edging up on the bunker, they ran out of ammunition. The sergeant, being in command, took it on himself to crawl back, strap new ammunition around his chest and then to return to his men. A Japanese sniper picked him out and shot into his ammunition which miraculously did not explode but burned instead with a flash, giving him a belt-like burn around his chest. At that moment he swore that he would give his right hand if he could get out of this hellish mess. He got out of it and now had to sacrifice the use of his right hand, which became paralyzed.

While telling the story, the sergeant spoke with great emotion, under terrific stress, wildly gesturing with his right hand, which he finally dropped motionless to his side when he had finished. Everybody noticed it and nobody said a word. Nobody took it on himself to catch the sergeant. Had he been confronted at that moment with the hysterical nature of his conversion, this might have caused him to slip into a psychotic episode. It was as if the entire group sensed that. The sergeant needed only a few days to give up the paralysis of his hand.

A FALSE PROPHET

I used to have a man in one of my groups who was by far the youngest of the group. He was a sportsman who liked football and other strenuous exercise. He was no longer successful in his career and wanted to understand what was happening to him. He was unsophisticated, even though he had a good, natural intelligence and was alert and fast in this thinking. One day he surprised us all with his pointed wit and even more with the high degree of correctness in his responses and in his freely given interpretations, all exactly to the point. I reacted to this with recognition and praise. Later somebody else joined in the praise with the words: "Are you sharp today!" And finally another psychiatrist, a member of the group, was startled and reacted with loud appreciation.

The young man sat back, looked at the ceiling and said; "Here I am in a room full of experts and nobody recognizes that I am so stoned that I cannot see straight."

The point of this observation is that everybody is a therapist but that sometimes it takes peculiar methods to bring the therapeutic gifts of a member into full bloom.

I had seen a similar phenomenon in another one of my groups. Alfred, a surgeon, had been born in Europe during the war and brought up for four years, separated from his parents, who were living in hiding. He came to treatment because of almost constant headaches which he had had almost all his adult life. When his hostility was activated and understood he improved dramatically. Then his headaches returned to a much lesser degree, though they were still annoying.

During one session he revealed astonishing insight. After he had spoken in previous sessions about his hostility toward his parents by whom he felt rejected, he now changed to his fear of rejection and his constant invitation to be rejected. For instance, he always played down his considerable success in his profession so that his parents could not belittle it as he feared they would. He had advanced in his profession far earlier than would be expected. He was driven to succeed as a bribe to his parents: you must not reject me. Even his gambling was a gambling with fate and fortune, the winning was acceptance by the mother and the losing a rejection. The real gain was the reward by the mother to her child, not because he worked but just because she loved him.

His insight was truly astonishing. It seemed convincing and amounted to a deepened insight into everything he had learned. He then told us that all this insight had come to him when stoned.

14

Conducting Analytic Group Therapy as Growth Experience

Some aging therapists develop the belief that they are superior to all. Others may become bitter and cynical about the needs of their patients, or they become exhibitionistic and narcissistic, believing that everything is permitted as long as they do it. Others may become depressed or resigned. Their reputation may be affirmed by then and an encounter with these old men of therapy may still be worthwhile.

A group therapist is not a patient among patients, even when he allows himself occasionally to become a member of the group-family. If we deny ourselves this alliance with our groups, we are in danger of becoming rigid or lazy or old in the worst sense of the word, meaning of closed mind. We then deny ourselves an opportunity for growth, and the group would miss the encounter with a responsive and human therapist.

A therapist is mature when he has learned how to deal with the inner and outer reality of himself and his patients. He becomes wise when he has learned how to deal with the problem of aging and how to accept the existential facts of death and dying.

There is a difference between therapeutic benefit and learning. Therapists should not become a burden to the group. However, it is necessary for us to remain students among people who all want to learn how to live honestly. Our patients can show us how weak man is and how strong to fight his weakness. They can help us to new knowledge and insight no matter how young they are or how old or sick and how many years we have spent in our profession. As a Jewish proverb says, If you learn ONE good word from a fool, call him a *hochum* (wise man).

Sometimes it seems to me that people with a European background and upbringing find it somewhat easier to develop an effective therapeutic alliance with patients. I am talking about a specific European attitude which I had a chance to observe in the early days of the Berlin Institute of Psychoanalysis. Then we continued our discussions in the coffeehouses after the meetings and debated with enthusiasm, skill, joy, artistry, intensity, and guilt-free viciousness. We did not need enemies as long as we had friends.

It is this open hostility toward a friend which forms an essential part of any working alliance with a patient. We are not lovers, not even friends, to our patients. Neither are we enemies. A working relationship is a fighting and still affectionate relationship; the healthy ego of the patient fights together with the therapist against the bad, the evil, the sinful, and the sick. People who believe that one should not fight with a friend will have difficulty understanding the essence of a therapeutic alliance. One should fight only with friends.

In group therapy this attitude is a necessity; the group knows that without being told so. The group knows this as well as a healthy family in which the natural tendency to growth and maturation is based on infighting. It is a part of honest and spontaneous interaction. To exercise it can become a learning experience for the therapist.

I am often touched but also amazed when a therapist goes all out in his affection for a patient he hardly knows. I frequently need years before I get to that point. For me it heralds termination of therapy since the cutting edge of my critical attitude is the indication of my therapeutic efficiency. There are patients who do not understand this, and if the therapist is not aware of it, he may drive them to the drop-out point. In one such encounter one patient explained my behavior to a fellow group member with the words "Grotjahn fights for your soul, not for your affection."

When I compare my attitude over the years in the one-to-one relationship with my later developed attitude or responsive spontaneity in groups, then I realize that I have become more courageous and direct. Where I used to be diplomatic, or hesitant, I am now direct and open; where I used to ask a question, I make a statement now, anticipating that my patients will respond to it and, if necessary, correct me.

A frankly critical remark in the group will be heard and reacted to. The same remark in the one-to-one relationship might have been devastating and overwhelming. The person in the group feels stronger.

To obtain emotional freedom is the great benefit a therapist may gain when he conducts groups well. His example of giving to the group and taking from it is a model for everybody. Only in this sense does he become a member of the group and participant in the interaction. His response is an important addition to his interpretation.

The therapist needs strength and endurance for the necessary infighting of the group. He must have it to start with, and he will develop it further as he goes along. He must not be what a patient of mine once called a "hit and run therapist." These are therapists with a good intuitive sense for the patient's sensitive areas which they invade with speed and accuracy, but then they do not stand their ground and deepen the interpretation. Instead they retreat with equal speed. They prefer an easy peace to the necessary painful encounter. This does not give the patient time for working through, and what was intended to be a maturing experience may turn into a trauma followed by defensive measures which complicate further work. The loss is not exclusively that of the patient. The therapist too will lose since the process of working through moves in both directions between the antagonists.

A therapist who cannot look straight into the eyes of his group has not yet developed enough strength. There are, however, certain exceptions: insight, as the word implies, is inner vision. Sometimes when I want to look into the unconscious meaning of interaction, then I may close my eyes so that I may see better. In the language of the symbol, the seer of antiquity is blind or like Wotan has lost at least one eye, which is now inner directed.

The therapist may know fear but he is not allowed to retreat from it. He must learn how to use the power of sickening fear in order to ride on top of it to health.

It is an abuse of the therapeutic situation if the therapist presents himself as a fellow patient, as I know some therapists claim to do. However, it is an insult to the principle of honesty, frankness, and sincerity if the therapist is unwilling to offer his unconscious for the understanding by the group. He has to learn how to function between the two opposite errors of either becoming a burden to the group or trying to remain out of reach and aloof. The conductor of an orchestra plays no instrument, but it helps if he sometimes takes an instrument and shows how he wants it played at that moment.

The therapist is a technical expert. At times he is allowed to be a model-setting participant, even in responsive self-revelation. Sigmund Freud said once that one must remember the difference between "privata" and "privatissima."

It would be a peculiar family in which the mother or the father did not occasionally appeal for understanding.

My experience with my colleagues and myself shows me that it is easier to grow old gracefully as a group therapist than in the frightful isolation of an analyst. We do not need to abuse our groups as tools of treatment for ourselves, but we may accept the help of the group in the continuation of our self-analysis. Beethoven is supposed to have said: "If you understand my music you are saved." Applied to the therapeutic situation this means that when we are understood by our patients in our groups we have learned something and the group has benefited too. A family who understands its mother or father will have freed the way to further growth, maturation, and individuation. Parents, sometimes, learn and grow with their children, and so does the therapist grow with his patients. This apparently is given to him to a much larger extent through the group than in a one-to-one relationship, in which the patient is not a member of a family but stands alone like an only child. A family can deal with a father in doubt or rage, but an only child should not be a confidant.

One other theme is worked through to a deeper degree in groups than it is usually possible in the one-to-one relationship. Not only aging and sickness, but also death and dying can be discussed easier in groups than in analysis. Where there are two people involved, it almost always sounds, or feels, as if the one person talks about the death of the other one. Soon, the dialogue ends in guilt and silence.

In the group the associations about death and dying are felt deeply but are less guilt and anxiety producing than in the loneliness of the analytic situation. I am more and more convinced that the analysis of death anxiety has been neglected in psychotherapy. It is of greatest importance not only in psychotic conditions but quite generally.

One more advantage of the group in dealing with death and dying must be mentioned. In analysis when one of the two partners in the dialogue gets seriously ill or dies, it is the end of the analysis. It is not necessarily so in a group. If someone dies, we survivors have to deal with it, and the doors to discussing a most difficult theme are open wide. It would be a foolish therapist who closes them again. Not even the death of the therapist is necessarily the end of the group. I have experience with one such orphaned group who continued at first their work on the traumatic event of having lost their central figure through unexpected death and then continued to work on other unsettled issues.

There are also changes in a therapist's narcissistic orientation when he conducts analytic groups. Almost every aging analyst considers himself the best in his profession. He may do so loudly or silently. Perhaps this is a necessary illusion in our profession. It may be generally true even outside analytic work. A surgeon may have an equal need to consider himself as the best. Working with groups, the therapist will have to face the fact that everybody is at times a good therapist, women even more so than men. Women seem to identify with the image of the mother while men identify with the image of the son. The feminine, motherly attitude of understanding is the essence of the therapeutic attitude.

What at first feels like a blow to the therapist's narcissism later develops into confidence in the therapeutic impact of the group.

One peculiar clinical observation seemingly contradicts what was said here. It would seem logical that after a lifelong experience in our work, the veteran therapist should almost be the perfect man which he obviously is not. The character changes which result from the years of conducting analytic group therapy as outlined here are an abstraction and a hope. Their realization is endangered by so many human frailties that it is frequently not reached. The lifelong contact with one's own or other people's unconscious harbors dangers to mental health. To use them as challenge is the chance we have to grow with our work. To fail this challenge may lead to such pathologies as the Mother Superior complex of the young therapist, the conflicts about seduction and temptation of the middle-aged therapist, and the God complex of the senior therapist. Cynicism, depression, alienation, and isolation are other symptoms.

It is the assignment of the therapist to work his way through the dangers, challenges, and opportunities of his work, as though he were his own favorite patient.

Theodor Reik said once in his Sunday morning conversations with Erika Freeman that the analyst "analyzes the other person as if the other person were himself, and he analyzes himself as if he were another person in self-analysis."

15

Observations on
Training, Supervision
and Consultations

Psychoanalytic training has traditionally been a model for all training in psychotherapy, especially since World War II, when psychoanalysis came of age and so many psychiatrists returning from the war demanded intensive training. Psychoanalytic training also can be used as a warning. In my opinion every group therapist should go through psychoanalytic training; at the same time I hope that psychoanalytic training will be more clinical and less theoretical. The heart of training should be the student's analysis and later his analytic group experience.

SOME REMARKS ABOUT SUPERVISION

There are two stages of supervision: it is at first group-directed, and later will become therapist-directed.

A colleague asking for a consultation will show me in his free associative report his therapeutic skill, his frankness, and his honesty. If he reads from notes he does not allow himself to give the best picture of the situation. Notes are used to hide behind. I always visit my colleague in his office and observe him conducting his group sessions. An analytically trained therapist may often be shocked by this and claim that my visit would interfere with the transference situation. This is not the case.

According to my experience it is not possible to give more than an anecdotal impression of the group situation or the group process to the consultant. My colleague can state his problem or describe the symptoms of a stalemate, a slowdown, or other forms of resistance in the group process. The real life of the group, including the attitude of the therapist, has to be witnessed by the consultant himself. He has to learn how to function as a participant observer, which is not always easy. I have seen consultations in which the therapist just sat back as if the conduct of this group were the responsibility of the visiting consultant.

Video tape is certainly an important aid in understanding the group process, however, it is still a substitute for the living participation or an addition to it. Using video tape is like performing in front of mirrors. Nobody wants to live without mirrors, and nobody feels comfortable when he lives constantly in front of mirrors.

The great advantage of witnessing a video tape of one's own performance is that it shows conflict-free areas of the ego of which we are not aware and which can be quite influential in the conduct of the group. I, for instance, am not fully aware of my accent. In the first minute of listening to a video tape I am shocked to hear my outspoken German accent which is still so strong after having spoken practically nothing else but English for forty years. Also, the handling of my monocle is something of which I am not aware and which emphasizes considerably certain aspects of my behavior and interaction. I noticed further that I use my hands to point, to encourage, to hold back, to emphasize and to question. On video tape I look like a conductor who has lost his baton.

Beginning therapists are often happy if they can start any kind of action or interaction in their groups. This implies that they are turning to the loudest and most confusing or, and this is especially dangerous, to the most provocative, debating and argumentative patients. I have been inclined to accept this technique in the beginning but of late I have become sensitive to schizophrenic patients who try to monopolize and therefore endanger the group process. To establish some kind of relationship among schizophrenics is more important than a loud and dramatic, but usually empty, excitement.

THE TWO MOST MEANINGFUL
CONSULTATIONS

I never saw any therapist who defended note-taking during group sessions, not even the therapist who fills notebooks during individual interviews. However, I find it most helpful to report briefly about every group meeting after the session. This is a consultation with one's self and a training in self-observation. As an analyst should occasionally write down his dreams which usually suffices to understand them, so the group therapist should regularly report about the group process.

There is one other method of consultation which I find most helpful. In moments of annoyance, helplessness, or even despair during a group session, I may lean back in my chair and say, addressing nobody in particular; "What is wrong with us today? What happened? Nothing? Where did we derail?"

When I tried this cry for help once in a group of residents, I regretted it immediately because I heard nothing but hostile criticism of me. The group was not willing to look at itself. Freud's *Ur-Horde* had a chance to murder the father.

I asked the same question once in another group and got a shocking but honest and helpful answer: this is the way we are. We are a bunch of utterly unrelated, narcissistic people. You have to be patient with us.

In other, differently structured groups, the members located the roadblock and then we moved again. These are moments when one can see group resistance.

FORGIVABLE AND UNFORGIVABLE
MISTAKES I HAVE SEEN

The group is a kind patient. The group forgives many mistakes and may react to them or point them out. A mistake becomes unforgivable in terms of the group process only when it is repeated, enforced, and not corrected.

Occasionally it happens to me that I forget, interchange, or make mistakes with the names of group members. As a rule this is loudly corrected by the group. Sometimes, and especially when I compare the dynamics of one patient with the dynamics of another in order to illustrate similarities or differences, then a mistake in the name can be quite confusing and annoying and sometimes devastating. If at all possible I try to analyze my slip immediately, following the early tradition of analysts.

People not accustomed to this instant analysis will look almost automatically for hostile motivations when interchanging names or using wrong ones. Although a hostile motivation is frequent it is by no means the only motive. I occasionally use the same name from one group to another for the person who sits in a specific spot, let us say, in the next chair to my right. The reason for sitting there often is similar for different people. They want to become my right hand man. I may use the name of the man whom I consider most fitted to be my right hand man for all of them.

I may call a patient with the name of another and my analysis of the mistake often leads me to the insight that I wish one patient to be as intelligent, as helpful, or as insightful as the patient whose name I mistakenly used.

Hidden hostility may well be a frequent motive. For instance, I had one patient whom I lost because she tried to dominate the group in an unpardonable way by trying to interfere, interpret, protect, or attack. I insisted that this behavior would have to stop and when it did not, the patient left the group to everybody's relief. For a while after that, whenever I saw similar behavior it could almost be predicted that I would call her with the name of this patient.

I made a tragic mistake when I addressed a young woman with the name of her mother who had recently died. The patient was startled but did not say anything. It gave me a moment's thought, but then I had to follow the group process and forgot the incident. Shortly thereafter I made the same mistake a second time and now the patient reacted with justifiable annoyance and said: "Do you hate me? Do you want me to die as mother did?" I needed a few moments before I could respond, "I am sure I do not want you to die, but there are parts in you which are unacceptable to you and to me and to everybody. I want these parts to die so that the good part, the acceptable part of you, may live."

THE MOST FREQUENTLY OBSERVED MISTAKE

I am in favor of analytic training and consider psychoanalysis as the basis of all dynamic psychiatry and therapy. It is, however, a mistake when an analytically trained therapist goes without experience and without additional training into the conduct of group psychotherapy. Such therapists are inclined to analyze individuals while the group witnesses the procedure. This is a mistake which I frequently had to combat in groups of psychiatrists, who when seeing a colleague in distress appointed themselves to a board of analysts analyzing their colleague. Occasionally such an occurrence is unavoidable. It may even be successful in rare situations, but soon it is time to point out definitely and repeatedly that in a well-conducted analytic group spontaneous response and interaction take priority over analyzing one single individual.

There is a second rule which has to be occasionally stated and which has to be kept in mind by the therapist at all times. An interpretation must not become a substitute for an emotion. The group has to feel first before they begin to understand what they are feeling. The group must learn to allow the growth of spontaneous emotion and to postpone interpretation.

We always make a mistake when we try to analyze somebody who does not belong to the group, for example the wife or a husband, the father or a mother of a patient.

There seem to be therapists who consider it their only duty to ask repeatedly, "How do you *feel?*" It seems to me that such a direct question kills most feeling. A certain skill is needed to make somebody volunteer to show his feelings. A direct question is only rarely indicated and leads usually to silence or meaningless words.

In one of my hospital groups, a deeply depressed woman talked about her despair. She wanted to sign up for unemployment insurance and failed to do so. She ran after want-ads and never got there in time; her car broke down and nobody was there to help. Her voice was choked and she began to cry. A big black woman symbolizing the mother of us all, responded and said, "Well, well, well, you sure hit rock bottom. I know how it feels. I have been there and I came out of it. I could not even keep my apartment clean which I can do now." She continued to talk in this warm, motherly way until the therapist almost rudely interrupted her and said: "But how do you really feel about the depression of this woman?" To me, the supervisor, this seemed a misleading question since both women had revealed deep feelings. So I said something like, "We cannot promise to love you, but we do care for you and that should make it a little easier. Several people here have been as low as you are, and now they are on the way up. That should give you some hope. That is what the group is doing for you."

16

Where I Am Today

I once gave a lecture about the meaning of being a psychiatrist – a man, after all, who makes a profession out of studying his fellow man and himself and who tries to understand why they are, what they are, and where they failed. I enumerated the dangers, mistakes, pitfalls, and disappointments which go with being an observer of the human scene while being human oneself. One of my listeners, a young man – and perhaps I should add that it was my son – asked me the decisive question: "And what did you get out of being a psychiatrist?" My answer came without hesitation, "I have lived seven-hundred lives – perhaps a thousand. I have been young and old, man and woman, son and father, happy and not so happy, manic, depressive, and even schizophrenic at times, at least in my dreams. I have been a German and an American, and finally I have become a citizen of the world. I have tried to become an existential man in charge of myself and in contact with my unconscious. This has given my life a new dimension."

I live the life of myself, my family, and my patients; I studied and thought and felt and reported about it to my friends, in case they wanted to read about it. All my writing was done in this way, just as I often wrote down my dreams, which as a rule sufficed to understand them. I must clarify my thoughts by reporting about them in my writing to my friends, colleagues, and students. Writing for me is a joyful post-graduate education.

All through my life I felt like a mountain guide who has climbed many mountains all over the world, alone or with my patients. The mountains, symbolizing the difficulties of human life, are still there, but by now some of us have become experts in climbing them while others got lost, gave up, or had to turn back.

Often I felt like a gardener, a modest gardener, who does not expect his cabbage to grow into roses, who knows that corn is corny, and who recognizes and loves an orchid when he sees one, perhaps once in a lifetime.

A healthy man is a free man who finally has the courage to be what he is. This is his virtue, and not to be it is his only sin and sickness. I still *hope to* get there before it is too late.

Bibliography

In the following reference list, books marked with an asterisk (*) are especially recommended reading as are the following journals.

International Journal for Group Psychotherapy. Important for anyone who wishes to remain in contact with progress and research in our field.

Group Analysis: International Panel for Correspondence. A lively exchange of letters, dialogues, discussions, controversies, book reviews, and other topics by many group analysts in the Western world.

*Anthony, J. 1968. Reflections on twenty-five years of group psychotherapy. *International Journal of Group Psychotherapy* 18:277–301. A beautifully written history of group therapy from a man who was there at its beginning.

Alexander, F. 1946. The principle of flexibility. In *Psychoanalytic Therapy,* ed. F. Alexander and T. French, pp. 25–65. New York: Ronald.

Bergen, M., and Rosenbaum, M. 1967. Notes on help-rejecting complainers. *International Journal of Group Psychotherapy* 47:357–370.

Berkovitz, I. 1972. *Adolescents Grow in Groups*. New York: Brunner/ Mazel.

Berne, E. 1955. Group attendance: clinical and theoretical considerations. *International Journal of Group Psychotherapy* 5:392–403.

Beukenkamp, C. 1956. Clinical observations on the effect of analytically oriented group therapy and group supervision on the therapist. *Psychoanalytic Review* 43:82–90.

———— 1958. *Fortunate Strangers*. New York: Rinehart.

Bion, W. R. 1952. Group dynamics: a review. *International Journal of Psycho-Analysis* 33:235–247.

*De Maré, P. 1972. *Perspectives in Group Psychotherapy*. New York: Jason Aronson. Written for any therapist interested in the theoretical aspects of group work.

*Durkin, H. E. 1964. *The Group in Depth*. New York: International Universities Press. A well-written, clinical description of group psychotherapy.

*Foulkes, S. H. 1964. *Therapeutic Group Analysis*. New York: International Universities Press. The founder of group analysis develops his basic concepts and techniques.

Freeman, E. 1971. *Insights: Conversations with Theodor Reik*. Englewood Cliffs, New Jersey: Prentice-Hall.

*Freud, S. 1921. Group psychology and the analysis of the ego. *Standard Edition* 18:67–144. Sigmund Freud's classic book on group psychology in relationship to the unconscious, without reference to therapy.

Garetz, C. 1971. Group rounds versus individual medical rounds on a psychiatric inpatient service. *American Journal of Psychiatry* 128:119–121.

Greenson, R. 1965. The working alliance and the transference neurosis. *Psychoanalytic Quarterly* 34:134–165.

Grotjahn, M. 1950. The process of maturation in group psychotherapy and in the group therapist. *Psychiatry* 13:63.

———— 1951. Special problems in the supervision of group psychotherapy. *Group Psychotherapy* 3:308.

———— 1960. *Psychoanalysis and the Family Neurosis*. New York: Norton.

———— 1969. Analytic group therapy with psychotherapists. *International Journal of Group Psychotherapy* 19:326–333.

———— 1971. The qualities of the group therapist. In *Comprehensive*

Group Psychotherapy, ed. H. L. Kaplan and B. J. Sadock, pp. 757–773. Baltimore: Williams and Wilkins.

_____ 1972. Learning from dropout patients: clinical view of patients who discontinued group psychotherapy. *International Journal of Group Psychotherapy* 22:306–318.

_____ 1975a. Growth experience in the leader. In *The Leader in the Group*, ed. by Z. A. Liff, pp. 146–150. New York: Jason Aronson.

_____ 1975b. The treatment of the famous and the beautiful people. In *Group Psychotherapy, 1975. An Overview*, ed. L. R. Wolberg and M. Aronson, pp. 76–82. New York: Stratton International.

*_____ 1976a. *The Art and Technique of Analytic Group Psychotherapy* (Cassette tape, T-638). New York: Psychotherapy Tape Library. Gives the main points of the clinical observations and opinions as described in this book.

_____ 1976b. A discussion of acting out incidents in groups. In *Group Therapy, 1976: An Overview*, ed. L. Wolberg and M. Aronson, pp. 180–186. New York: Stratton International.

Guntrip, H. 1968. *Schizoid Phenomena, Object Relations and the Self: The Developing Synthesis of Psychodynamic Theory*. New York: International Universities Press.

Heath, E. S., and Bacal, H. A. 1968. A method of group psychotherapy at the Tavistock Clinic. *International Journal of Group Psychotherapy* 18:21–31.

*Kanzer, M. 1971. Freud: the first psychoanalytic group leader. In *Comprehensive Group Psychotherapy*, ed. H. Kaplan and B. Sadock, pp. 32–47. Baltimore: Williams and Wilkins. A comprehensive coverage of the entire field of group therapy by many authors competent to write about their special field of research and experience.

Kaplan, H., and Sadock, B. 1971. *Comprehensive Group Psychotherapy*. Baltimore: Williams and Wilkins.

*Kreeger, M. 1975. *The Large Group*, London: Constable. A first attempt to describe large groups of 25 to 250 people.

Kline, F. 1972. Dynamics of leaderless groups. *International Journal of Group Psychotherapy* 22:234–242.

Kubie, L. 1968. Unsolved problems in the resolution of the transference. *Psychoanalytic Quarterly* 37:331–352.

McGee, T. F., and Schuman, B. N. 1970. The nature of the cotherapy relationship. *International Journal of Group Psychotherapy* 20:25–36.

Mahler, M. 1968. *On Human Symbiosis and the Vicissitudes of Individuation.* New York: International Universities Press.

Mullan, H., and Rosenbaum, M. 1962. *Group Psychotherapy.* Glencoe, IL: Free Press.

Moreno, J. 1954. Interpersonal therapy, group therapy and the function of the unconscious. *International Journal of Group Psychotherapy* 7:191–204.

Morgan, D. 1971. Psychoanalytic group psychotherapy for therapists and their wives. *International Journal of Group Psychotherapy* 21:244–247.

Pines, M. 1975. Overview: chapter 11. In *The Large Group,* L. Kreeger, pp. 291–312. London: Constable.

*Reik, T. 1948. *Listening With the Third Ear.* New York: Farrar, Straus and Giroux. A brilliant justification of intuition as a tool of therapy.

Rosenbaum, M., and Berger, M. 1968. *Group Psychotherapy and Group Function.* New York: Basic Books.

Ross, W., and Kapp, F. 1962. A technique for analysis of counter transference: use of the psychoanalyst's visual images in response to patient's dreams. *Journal of the American Psychoanalytic Association* 10:643.

Scheidlinger, S. 1968. The concept of regression in group psychotherapy. *International Journal of Group Psychotherapy* 18:3–20.

Schindler, W. 1951. Family pattern in group formation and therapy. *International Journal of Group Psychotherapy* 1:100–105.

_____ 1953. Countertransference in family-pattern group psychotherapy. *International Journal of Group Psychotherapy* 3:424–430.

_____ 1966. The role of the mother in group psychotherapy. *International Journal of Group Psychotherapy* 16:198–200.

Semrad, E. V., and Day, M. 1966. Group psychotherapy. *Journal of the American Psychotherapy Association* 14:519–618.

Skynner, R. 1976. *Systems of Family and Marital Psychotherapy.* Brunner/ Mazel.

Stein, A. 1952. Some aspects of resistance in group psychotherapy. *Journal of the Hillside Hospital* 1:79–88.

_____ 1963. Indications for group psychotherapy and the selection of patients. *Journal of the Hillside Hospital* 12:145–155.

Wahl, C. 1974. Psychotherapy of the rich, influential and famous people. *Contemporary Psychoanalysis* 10:71–85.

Winnicott, D. 1965. *The Maturational Processes and the Facilitating Environ-ment: Studies in the Theory of Emotional Development.* New York: International Universities Press.

Wolf, A. 1950. The psychoanalysis of groups. *American Journal of Psychotherapy* 3:525–558; 4:16–50.

*Yalom, I. 1970. *The Theory and Practice of Group Psychotherapy.* New York: Basic Books. A useful and practical outline of group therapy with numerous clinical illustrations.